# SAVE YOUR IDENTITY

## ID THEFT AWARENESS, PREVENTION, AND RECOVERY

# SAVE YOUR IDENTITY

MICHAEL CHESBRO

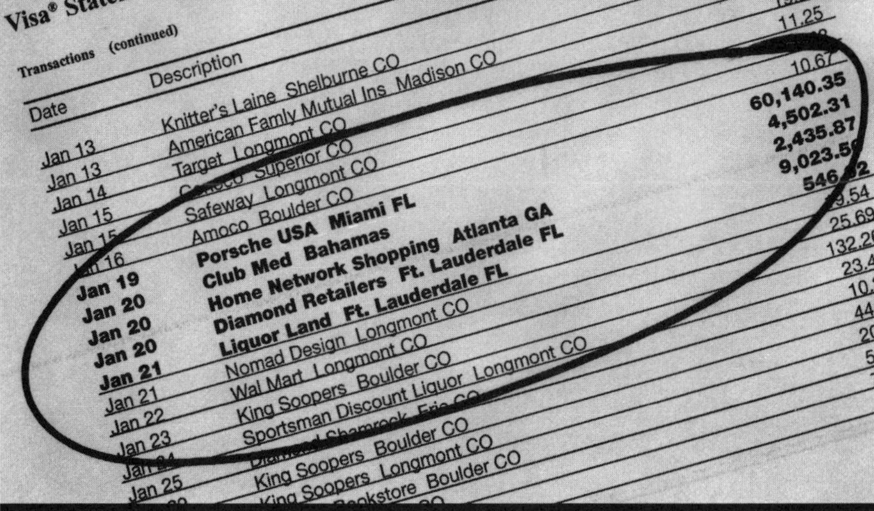


PALADIN PRESS • BOULDER, COLORADO

*Save Your Identity:*
*ID Theft Awareness, Prevention, and Recovery*
by Michael Chesbro



ISBN 1-58160-445-9
Printed in the United States of America

Published by Paladin Press, a division of
Paladin Enterprises, Inc.
Gunbarrel Tech Center
7077 Winchester Circle
Boulder, Colorado 80301 USA
+1.303.443.7250

Direct inquiries and/or orders to the above address.



Visit our Web site at www.paladin-press.com

# Table of Contents

# Introduction

We have all likely heard the term "identity theft," but just what is identity theft? How does someone steal your identity? Is identity theft really a problem? What can you do to protect yourself against it? If you become the victim of an identity thief, what can you do to mitigate the damage and recover your losses? This book will answer these questions. It will discuss things you can do *now* to help prevent becoming a victim of identity theft, and it will explain the steps you must take if you find that you have become a victim of identity theft, in order to mitigate the damage and recover from the crime.

In simple terms, identity theft is the appropriation of your personal identification information (i.e., name, date of birth, Social Security number) by someone other than you for criminal purposes. Federal law (18 U.S.C. Section 1028) defines an identity thief as someone who "knowingly transfers or uses, without lawful authority, a means of identification of another person with the intent to commit, or to aid or abet, any unlawful activity that constitutes a violation of Federal law, or that constitutes a felony under any applicable State or local law." An identity thief uses your personal information and pretends to be you. He may obtain a credit card, open a checking account, obtain cellular telephone service, or apply for a loan in your name. Given time, an identity thief may obtain government identification (e.g., driver's license or passport) in your name and even receive government services and benefits for which you may be held accountable. Every crime the identity thief commits using your identification points back to you. When he obtains a credit card in your name and runs up charges that he never pays, this is reflected on your credit report. When he opens a checking account in your name and writes thousands of dollars in checks, all of which bounce, the bank and the bill collectors will be looking for you. When he obtains a driver's license in your name and thereafter fails to pay some traffic ticket, it will be your name on the bench warrant issued by a judge.

All of these things and more can happen to you if you become the victim of identity theft. But just how likely is it that you will become a victim of this crime?

## IS IT REALLY THAT BIG OF A PROBLEM?

Identity theft is a growing crime that is approaching epidemic proportions in the United States. In 2001 identity theft was the most common complaint filed with the Federal Trade Commission (FTC), comprising 42 percent of all complaints filed. In approximately 1,300 of the reported cases, the victims of identity theft were subjected to criminal investigation, arrest, and even conviction for crimes committed by the identity thief using the victim's identity. The inspector general of the Social Security Administration, James Huse Jr., has labeled identity theft a "national crisis." In 1992, the credit reporting agency TransUnion received about 35,000 calls from victims of identity theft and those concerned about this crime. In 2001, it received more than 1 million such calls. In a lecture given on December 7, 2000, Jim Kerins, president of the National Fraud Center (NFC), a division of the Lexis-Nexis Risk Solutions Group, stated, "Identity theft continues to grow in the virtual environment of e-commerce. In this setting, fraud and risk losses have increased substantially, to more than $1 billion." James E. Bauer, deputy assistant director of the Office of Investigations, U.S. Secret Service, has stated, "Identity takeover fraud has come into its own and promises not to go away until significant changes evolve in the manner and methods by which personal identifiers are collected and used."

Identity theft is not some infrequently occurring crime that we can afford to ignore, nor is it something that just happens to someone else. According to the technology research organization The Gartner Group, there is likely to be "mass victimization" by identity thieves. CBS News.com, reporting on identity theft on January 29, 2001, warned, "This year alone more than 500,000 Americans will be robbed of their identities . . . with more than $4 billion stolen in their names."

According to a study conducted by The Gartner Group, "An Internet survey of more than 1,000 adult U.S. online consumers conducted in January 2002 showed that 5.2 percent of respondents were victimized by credit card fraud in 2001 and 1.9 percent were victimized by identity theft (although respondents do not know whether the theft occurred online or offline)."

By May 2003 identity theft made the Top-10 list of security threats facing U.S. businesses, according to the Pinkerton Consulting and Investigations 10th Annual Survey of Fortune 1000 Corporate Security Professionals.

In May 2002 the Privacy Rights Clearinghouse released the

results of its survey of identity theft victims. The survey revealed that the average victim spends 175 hours and more than $800 to resolve problems caused by identity theft and that it can take between two and four years to get these problems cleared up. It is important to recognize that 175 hours is more than a month of full-time work, figuring a 40-hour workweek. The $800 is *not* reimbursed; it comes out of *your* pocket and is gone—the monetary price you pay to clear up the effects of being a victim of identity theft. Furthermore there is a two- to four-year period during which you have errors in your credit reports; bill collectors are calling you; you have problems receiving credit, applying for a loan, and mortgaging a home; and you may be defending yourself against various criminal and civil charges.

Identity theft can go on for months or even years before you become aware that you are a victim. When an identity thief is running up debt in your name, you may not be aware of it until you apply for some type of credit yourself. Perhaps you decide it's time to buy that new car or dream home, and the price is well within what you can afford. Maybe your kid is ready to begin his or her first year of college. So you go to your bank and apply for a loan. You know that you've always paid your bills on time and that you've used credit responsibly for several years, so you're expecting quick approval of your loan application. It comes as quite a shock when your loan application is turned down cold. *Denied!* Your credit reports show thousands of dollars in bad debt, massive late payments, or simply no payments at all with accounts being closed and sent to collection agencies. You're the victim of an identity thief. There will be no new car this year. That dream home will go to someone else since you can't get financing, and your child will be flipping burgers at the local fast food restaurant because you can't get a loan to cover college tuition this year.

Finally, consider the findings of Congress as presented in Senate Bill S223—The Identity Theft Prevention Act (108th Congress, 1st Session, 28 January 2003):

## Introduction

Congress finds that—

(1) the crime of identity theft has become one of the major law enforcement challenges of the new economy, as vast quantities of sensitive, personal information are now vulnerable to criminal interception and misuse;

(2) in November 2002, Americans were alerted to the dangers of identity theft when Federal prosecutors announced that 3 individuals had allegedly sold the credit and personal information of 30,000 people, the largest single identity theft case in United States history;

(3) hundreds of thousands of Americans are victims of identity theft each year, resulting in an annual cost to industry of more than $3,500,000,000.

(4) several indicators reveal that despite increased public awareness of the crime, the number of incidents of identity theft continues to rise;

(5) in December 2001, the Federal Trade Commission received an average of more than 3,000 identity theft calls per week, a 700 percent increase since the Identity Theft Data Clearinghouse began operation in November 1999;

(6) allegations of Social Security number fraud increased by 500 percent between 1998 and 2001, from 11,000 to 65,000;

(7) a national credit reporting agency reported that consumer requests for fraud alerts increased by 53 percent during fiscal year 2001;

(8) identity theft violates the privacy of American citizens and ruins their good names;

(9) victims of identity theft may suffer restricted access to credit and diminished employment opportunities, and may spend years repairing the damage to credit histories caused by identity theft;

(10) businesses and government agencies that handle sensitive personal information of consumers have a responsibility to protect this information from identity thieves; and

(11) the private sector can better protect consumers by implementing effective fraud alerts, affording greater consumer access to credit reports, truncating of credit card numbers, and establishing other prevention measures.

The foregoing information and much more like it, which can easily be discovered through an online or library search, should convince even the most skeptical person that Americans face a very serious and growing problem in the crime of identity theft. Once you concede that identity theft is a serious problem, you will want to take steps to prevent yourself from becoming a victim. In order to do this, you need to understand just how someone goes about stealing your identity.

## HOW DOES SOMEONE STEAL YOUR IDENTITY?

To steal your identity, an identity thief must know something about you. Unfortunately, he does not need to know a great deal. Just a few key pieces of information are all he needs. With nothing more than your name, date of birth, current address, and the key to identity theft—your Social Security number—a criminal can assume your identity.

Once a criminal is able to gather some basic information about you, he uses this information to convince others that he is you—that is, he steals your identity. This can run the gamut from something as simple as stealing your checkbook and forging checks to make purchases at local stores to completely assuming your identity over a period of months or years. In either case, however, in order to be successful the identity thief must know enough about you to convince someone else that he is in fact you. Unfortunately, this isn't all that difficult.

When you choose to disclose certain personal information to a business for a particular purpose (such as opening an account), too often you disclose the exact information needed by an identity thief, with little thought for the risk you assume every time you do so. Furthermore, adding insult to injury, the business often turns around and sells your personal and private information to other companies as part of its marketing scheme.

If you have established credit, a bit of money in savings, and perhaps some investments, it is easy to understand why an identity thief would target you as his next victim. He wants to steal your cash and make a fast getaway. On the other hand, it may be that you don't have any investments, no real savings, and haven't established much credit. Does this mean that you are safe? Will an identity thief ignore you because you have nothing he can steal immediately? Unfortunately, the answer to this question is a definite NO! You are also a potential target. An identity thief may take over your identity on a long-term basis and—because you are not actively using credit, are not maintaining a bank account, and the like—do a great deal of damage acting in your name before you ever become aware of the crime.

An identity thief will target anyone about whom he can discover sufficient personal information to make his crime successful. To protect yourself from the crime of identity theft, it is essential that you maintain your personal privacy. An identity thief will be hard-pressed to steal your identity if he can discover no personal information about you. Protect your personal information, and you will not become one of the hundreds of thousands of victims of identity theft every year.

As we continue to look at this crime, we will divide it into two overlapping categories: short-term identity theft and long-term identity theft.

## Short-Term Identity Theft

The short-term identity thief is after a quick score. He wants to grab as much of your money as he can in the shortest possible time and then move on to his next victim. The short-term identity thief will take over a portion of your identity, run up bills in your name, and then disappear.

An example of a short-term identity thief is the criminal who steals your wallet. He of course takes whatever cash you have, but he is also now in possession of your credit card(s) and identification. Using your credit cards, he quickly purchases several items that can easily be pawned or sold. He uses your credit cards until they are denied—because you have reported them stolen, or because he has run the credit limit to the maximum on them. Either way, as soon as one of your credit cards is denied, the thief simply abandons it.

An identity thief may also take over your checking account by stealing your checkbook and identification. Many businesses will accept personal checks as payment for their products or services. Some businesses will even cash checks for individuals who are not making a purchase. There are "check cashing" companies that make a business out of cashing checks, taking a percentage of the check as the fee for cashing it. It takes little effort to find one of these check-cashing services, and not much more to find one that requires little in the way of identification in order to cash a check. In fact, I have frequently seen these companies advertising "Checks Cashed Here—No ID Needed."

Even in cases where identification is required as a condition of cashing a check or making a purchase with a personal check, the ID check is often more of a formality than a function of security. If the name on the check matches the name on the ID presented, this is usually sufficient. There is usually little effort made to ensure that the ID matches the person presenting it or that it is not a forgery.

While researching this book, I accompanied a friend to a local shopping mall where he planned to make a few purchases. He had his personal checkbook and driver's license for identification. After finding the items he intended to purchase, he gave me his checkbook and driver's license, and I took his items to the checkout, where I attempted to make the purchase using his personal checks and ID. We tried this in three separate stores. In the two stores where I was actually asked for ID, I filled out the check and handed it to the cashier along with my friend's driver's license. In both cases the cashier looked at the driver's license and appeared to compare the information on the driver's license with that on the check.The cashier then returned the driver's license to me and thanked me for shopping at the store, and I was on my way with the purchases. In the third store, the cashier accepted my (friend's) check without even asking for any type of ID.

In each of these cases, had I been a thief I would have successfully made purchases, each totaling more than $50, with forged checks. It should be noted that, aside from being of the same basic age and build, I do not bear a close resemblance to my friend. Nor am I a skilled forger who was able to match my friend's signature from his driver's license when I signed his checks. I simply signed his name—the signatures did not really match.

You may be wondering why I was able to make purchases so easily using someone else's checking account and identification. The answer is simply *customer service*. Retail service personnel, salesmen, cashiers, and the like are trying to make sales and encourage repeat business. They are not security experts, and they generally are not considering the possibility of fraud during a transaction. While making these purchases I was neatly dressed. I was courteous to the cashier and made the usual small talk while my purchases were being totaled and while I wrote out the check to pay for them. In the first two instances the name and address on the driver's license I presented matched the name and address on the check I had just written. Even if these cashiers noticed some discrepancy, neither mentioned it. No cashier wants to accuse someone of presenting a forged check and take a chance on being wrong.

It's safe to assume that sooner or later an identity thief attempting to pass forged checks will run into a cashier who will call attention to a discrepancy or refuse to accept a check. However, this is usually not much of a problem for the identity thief. He simply gathers his forged check and stolen ID and leaves the store. The retail clerk has prevented the identity thief from making this one purchase, but there is almost no chance of this clerk notifying the police and having them look into possible check forgery or identity theft. Having refused to accept the forged check, the clerk/business has avoided being victimized, and thus the police—even if they were to be called, which is unlikely—probably will not do much.

This same type of misuse can be seen with credit cards. As long as the credit card successfully processes, it is rare for any merchant to question the transaction. It is so common for people to loan their credit cards to others (husbands/wives, boyfriends/girlfriends, parents/children) that if a customer has a credit card in other than his own name it is no longer a clear indicator of misuse.

Furthermore, credit card users too often fail to sign their cards, or they write some ridiculous statement, like "See ID" in place of their signature. As a result, retail clerks do not tend to compare signatures on the credit card and charge slip as part of the transaction.

When it comes to short-term identity theft, the identity thief will usually take over accounts that you have legitimately established (e.g., credit cards, checking accounts) and use them (pretending to be you) until he has depleted all available funds or is denied access because you have closed the accounts.

Short-term identity theft is a serious problem, but the damage is usually limited to loss of funds and disruption of specific accounts. While the effects of short-term identity theft can be disruptive, long-term identity theft can be disastrous.

## Long-Term Identity Theft

The long-term identity thief can take over your identity, posing as you for months or even years. He is looking for more than just a quick "score" and a little fast cash. He is using your identity to hide his own and will take actions in your name, such as obtaining credit cards, establishing accounts, and perhaps even making major purchases, such as an automobile. When he defaults on these debts, not only is your credit rating destroyed and your reputation ruined, but you can also be arrested and jailed!

One of the major differences is that while the short-term identity thief is taking over accounts you have established, the long-term identity thief is establishing new accounts in your name.

There are several reasons that an identity thief might take over your identity on a long-term basis. The first, of course, is the same as that of the short-term identity thief—he is trying to rip you off. The identity thief wants to steal your money (or steal money in your name), and he has a plan to do it. In this case, however, he is willing to invest some extra time and effort for a "bigger score."

A long-term identity thief may also choose to take over your identity in an effort to cover his own tracks—to hide his true identity behind yours. You need not be anybody special to qualify. In fact, the more mundane, run-of-the-mill life you lead, the more attractive you are to this type of identity thief. He will almost certainly run up bills in your name and then skip out on the unpaid debts, but in the interim he is looking to live his life as someone else—and that someone is you.

Having learned some basic information about you and having obtained your Social Security number (the key to identity theft), he will begin to gather identifying documents in your name for the purpose of establishing new accounts.

Let's see how this might work.

First, the identity thief needs to gain some form of basic ID in your name. This need not be anything too complicated, just something that can be flashed for those unofficial requests for ID. As we will see elsewhere in this book, there are places where one can purchase a convincing "novelty ID" for very little money. If our identity thief has a computer and good printer, he can even produce an acceptable ID at home with a little time and effort.

Having this basic ID in hand, our identity thief begins to

acquire additional documentation and services in your name. He might set up cellular telephone service, for instance, filling out the application using your identifying information and giving your Social Security number. The cellular company may run a credit check before establishing the account, but since the identity thief has provided your information (assuming you are not a total deadbeat), the account is going to be approved.

The identity thief might also set up an account with the local video rental store. Not much effort is required here, and the video rental card gives him a secondary piece of ID in your name. How about a "preferred shopper" card from one of the major grocery stores? The idea is to gather all those pieces of secondary identification and other clutter that you have in your wallet or purse.

As the identity thief continues to take over your identity, he will need a place to receive mail in your name. Establishing a mailing address is not an overwhelming problem for the identity thief by any means. One very simple way is to place a mailbox in line with others along a rural route or country road. Once the identity thief has set up his new box, the postal carrier will leave some forms for him to complete but may never actually see any house associated with the box. He or she is not going to search all of the twists and turns of backcountry roads to locate the house associated with a mailbox alongside the road. Once this "mailbox address" is established, it appears, for all intents and purposes, to be just another home along the rural delivery route, and the mail carrier will begin delivering mail to it.

Once he has established a mailing address, he can begin to set up even more accounts in your name. Department store credit cards, check cashing cards, fuel cards, calling cards—all can be obtained with no more than a basic ID and maybe a quick credit check. Remember, the identity thief has your Social Security number, so these checks are run using *your* name and approval is granted based on *your* credit rating.

With a mailing address, a basic ID in your name, and maybe a couple of department store credit cards in hand, the identity thief goes to the bank and opens a checking account. Now, the bank will almost certainly conduct a couple of basic checks when opening the account, but since these are being conducted in your name, and since the identity thief is putting money *in* the bank, he will have very little problem getting the account established.

The ease with which an identity thief can steal your identity is based upon only a couple of factors. First, people tend to believe what they see and hear unless given a specific reason to question it. If someone introduces himself as John Smith, you will recognize that person as being John Smith. When someone writes a check in the name of Sally Smith and shows you an ID card in the name of Sally Smith, you will likely believe that Sally is the one making payment with the check in question. Secondly, when basic credit checks are conducted, they tend to be keyed to a single identifying factor—the Social Security number. Such checks provide almost no security and almost always create an avenue by which an identity thief can gain access to your private records. This is why the Social Security number has rightly been called the key to identity theft.

So because the identity thief has gained access to your Social Security number, and because people tend to believe what they see and hear, he has been able to establish accounts and services in your name with little effort. Now he can continue to live his life under your name, and, assuming that he doesn't simply run up the accounts he has established to their maximum and skip town, you won't even be aware of it. As far as the creditors are concerned, he is you—and if he is paying the bills on time, they think you are paying the bills on time.

So why would an identity thief open accounts in your name and bother to pay the bills? Well, small accounts with low credit limits can lead to large accounts with high credit limits. Additionally, the identity thief may be using your identity to shield his true identity while he commits other types of crimes.

It is certainly safe to presume, however, that there will come a time when the identity thief will be ready to abandon your identity. This may be because he has maxed out all the credit cards he has obtained in your name, overdrawn any accounts he has established in your name, and finds that the services he has obtained in your name are being canceled for failure to pay. It may be that he finds the law looking for him (you?) and decides that your identity is no longer profitable. So he abandons your identity, leaving your credit in ruins, your good name sullied, and a number of bill collectors and maybe the police looking for you.

If this sounds extreme, remember that nearly 1 million people become the victims of identity theft every year. It has happened to them, and it can happen to you. But there are steps you can take to minimize the likelihood of becoming a victim—or mitigate the damage if you do.

# 1 Minimizing Your Risk

It is important to remember that identity theft is a crime, and, as with any crime, there are steps you can take to minimize your risk of becoming a victim. Everything you do to make it more difficult for a criminal to target you increases the likelihood that he will move on to someone who is less aware and less prepared. Just as you take precautions—such as locking the doors to your home—to protect yourself from burglars, you need to take precautions to protect yourself from identity thieves.

The first step in protecting yourself from identity theft is awareness. You must realize that this crime exists, that it is an increasing threat, and that you may become a victim if you don't take precautions against it. Since you are reading this book, we can assume that you already have an awareness of this threat, or at least you will once you finish reading it. The next step is to do those things that minimize the threat. Finally, should you be targeted by an identity thief despite those efforts, you can take action to mitigate the damage.

The essential element of identity theft prevention is maintaining your personal privacy. An identity thief cannot steal your identity if he can't discover certain basic information about you. If you make a habit of protecting your personal privacy, of not disclosing information about yourself, and of putting blocks in the way of others attempting to gather information about you, you can protect yourself from the crime of identity theft.

## IDENTITY THEFT PREVENTION TOP 10 LIST

There are many things you can do to prevent identity theft, and we will discuss these in detail throughout this book. There are, however, certain things that everyone should do right now that will significantly reduce the risk of identity theft. In researching this book, I have condensed these actions to a list of 10 essential steps.

1. Never disclose your Social Security number unless specifically required to by law. Remember, the Social Security number has become a de facto national identity number. If an identity thief can gain access to your Social Security number, he has the key to your identity.
2. Maintain only minimal information on your personal checks. You should only use personal checks to send money through the mail in order to pay established accounts. Never use personal checks to pay for a direct retail purchase.
3. Receive mail only in a locked box. Send mail only by depositing it at the post office. Mail theft is directly

associated with identity theft. Don't allow a thief to steal your identity by stealing your mail.

4. Don't provide supplementary identification when making a purchase with a credit card. The major credit card companies prohibit merchants from requiring ID as a condition of using a properly signed credit card. Merchants who do so are putting *you* at risk. Properly sign your credit cards, and don't show ID when using them.
5. Never deal with telemarketers or respond to unsolicited commercial e-mail (spam). When you provide personal information to telemarketers, you have no real proof that they are who they claim to be, and if you respond to spam you will find that it is almost always a scam.
6. Check your credit reports at least once per year. It is important to know what information is contained in your credit reports and to ensure that the information is accurate.
7. Establish a password on each of your accounts. Arrange for this password to be required before any information is given out about that account.
8. Opt out of all marketing and prescreening databases. Register with the Direct Marketing Association's (DMA's) Mail and Telephone Preference Services, and then opt out of the screening of your credit reports by calling 1-888-5-OPT-OUT.
9. Use a cross-cut paper shredder to destroy sensitive personal information before discarding it. Don't enable an identity thief to gather information about you by collecting your trash.
10. Protect your personal communication with strong encryption. Don't let your e-mail or online shopping become a source of information for an identity thief. Use encryption software such as Pretty Good Privacy

(PGP) to safeguard your e-mail, and shop online only on secure Web sites.

By following the above 10 steps, you will significantly reduce your vulnerability to identity theft. However, in order to safeguard yourself most effectively against identity theft and related crimes, it is necessary to examine the crime of identity theft and your vulnerabilities in greater detail.

# 2

# Factors Contributing to Identity Theft

There are many factors that contribute to identity theft, and any combination of them can lead to your becoming a victim. However, broadly speaking, the two leading causes are (1) failure of individuals to safeguard their personal information from unnecessary disclosure and (2) the collection by businesses and organizations of personal information that is not directly and immediately required for their daily operations and places their customers at risk for identity theft should that information be compromised.

Let's take a look at some specific examples of such security breaches and how they enable someone to steal your identity.

## MAIL THEFT

> *"For the criminal, the mailbox is the gateway to financial fraud, and victims are left with emptied bank accounts and shattered credit ratings."*
>
> —King County, Washington, Prosecuting Attorney Norm Maleng

Although "high-tech" theft of personal information contained in supposedly secure databases tends to make the national news, it is important to understand that for the most part identity theft is a fairly "low-tech" affair.

One common way for an identity thief to gather information about you (and thereafter use it against you) is to steal your mail. If you have your mail delivered to your home or leave it in an unlocked mailbox at your home to be picked up by your postal carrier, it is vulnerable to being stolen. Numerous agencies, organizations, and communities echo this warning. For example, the official Web site of the City of Lakewood, Colorado (www.lakewood.org), warns, "Identity theft occurs when a thief steals your personal identifying information to take over your bank accounts or fraudulently apply for credit in your name. The most common identifiers used are name, address, date of birth, Social Security number and mother's maiden name. *The majority of identity theft schemes involve the U.S. Mail* [emphasis added]."

Your unsecured mail is a gold mine for an identity thief. He can steal your new or renewed credit cards. He can steal your latest order of checks. He can steal your bank statement or your bills to obtain information about you and your accounts. This is not a minor or limited threat; in fact, mail theft is on the rise as indicated by regular news headlines:

"Identity Thefts on the Rise in Area, Postal Inspectors Say"
—*Dallas Morning News*, June 2002

## Factors Contributing to Identity Theft

"Two Charged with 445 Counts of Theft in Mailboxes Case"
—*Tampa Tribune*, 12 March 2002

"Women Charged with Stealing from Mailboxes across Gulf Coast"
—*The Tuscaloosa News*, 18 May 2002

"Postal Inspector Urges Everyday Precautions against Identity Theft"
—*Lubbock Avalanche-Journal*, 15 February 2002

Fay Faron, nationally recognized private investigator and columnist, stated in her column on 7 April 2002, "Mail is at its most vulnerable when placed in a residential mailbox. To leave it there unattended and unlocked is to trust every stranger that passes by your home—NOT SMART."

The U.S. Postal Inspection Service points out some basic facts about mail theft:

- Thieves often break into mailboxes at night and take advantage of customers who don't pick up their mail.
- Thieves know very well to look for mailboxes with the red flags up, and they'll quickly steal the mail.
- Mail thieves look for items found every day in the mail, such as bank statements and credit card bills, which they can use to create counterfeit checks or fake IDs. They also look for personal checks, such as utility bills or other payments, which they can "wash" clean of handwriting and fill in with new amounts—and make out to themselves. Check your financial statements regularly.
- We call them "dumpster divers"—thieves who go through trash bins looking for mail and any other information they can use to access your financial accounts or sell to someone else who wants to access your accounts. Shred all of your personal information before throwing it away.

The Postal Inspection Service (www.usps.gov/ postalinspectors/safemail.htm) then recommends the following steps to protect your mail:

- Place mail for pick-up in a blue collection box or at your post office.
- Pick up your mail promptly after delivery. Don't leave it in your mailbox overnight.
- Don't send cash in the mail.
- Ask your bank for "secure" checks that can't be altered.
- Tell your post office when you'll be out of town so they can hold your mail until you return.
- Report all mail theft to a postal inspector.

Protecting the security of your mail is an essential step in protecting yourself from identity theft. As we have seen, mail theft is one of the many crimes an identity thief will commit in order to steal your identity.

While First Class Mail is acceptable for most correspondence, you may want to consider more secure forms of mail for sensitive and important correspondence. Don't forget about services such as Priority Mail with delivery confirmation, Certified Mail, and Registered Mail. Although these services come at a premium price, they do provide additional security, confirmation, and tracking of your important and sensitive correspondence.

Simply put, you need to safeguard your outgoing mail by depositing it at the post office or in an official USPS mailbox. Mail you receive should be delivered to a post office box. If you have mail delivered to your home, it must be delivered to a locking mailbox. To do otherwise simply gives an identity thief the chance to use your mail as a source of information to steal your identity.

## DUMPSTER DIVING

*"We call them 'dumpster divers'—thieves who go through trash bins looking for mail and any other information they can use to access your financial accounts, or to sell to someone else who wants to access your accounts."*

—U.S. Postal Inspection Service

An identity thief can steal your mail without taking it from your mailbox. He can steal it from your trash bin! Unless you're a celebrity, you probably haven't thought much about anyone going through your trash, but your trash contains a treasure trove of information about you.

Sooner or later the bank statements, credit card statements, bills and invoices, preapproved offers for this and that, and pretty much everything else you receive in the mail will end up in your trash. Additionally, your trash contains information that would not be available to an identity thief who only stole your mail. Remember, not every piece of important, personal, or private information comes through the mail. For example, your paycheck and its associated pay stub may be given to you directly by your employer every payday. An identity thief getting a copy of your carelessly discarded pay stub would obtain a good deal of personal information about you.

Fortunately, preventing an identity thief from gaining any useful information from your trash is fairly easy to accomplish. It is simply a matter of ensuring that anything containing printed information is rendered into an unreadable format before you throw it away. Generally this means buying a paper shredder and using it to shred any documents, letters, bills, invoices, mailing labels, notes, and so on before throwing them into the trash.

Most office supply stores and many general department stores sell paper shredders. They come in two basic types: strip shredders and cross-cut shredders. Strip shredders cut the paper being shredded into continuous strips about a quarter-inch wide for the entire length of the paper. Cross-cut shredders cut the paper being shredded into strips and then cut each of these strips at a different angle to the original cut, resulting in small flakes of paper. Although either type will probably be sufficient to convince an identity thief to focus his efforts elsewhere, the cross-cut shredder is more secure (it provides more complete destruction of the shredded document) and should be used whenever possible.

Of course, one of the best ways to avoid having to shred large amounts of paper containing personal information is not to receive it in the first place. As we have already discussed, you can opt out of the screening of your credit report for "preapproved credit offers" by calling 1-888-5-OPT-OUT. Another way to limit the amount of junk mail you receive and the number of mass-marketing databases in which your personal information is contained is to register with the DMA's Mail Preference Service. Simply send a written request to the following address:

**Direct Marketing Association**
Attn: Mail Preference Service
P.O. Box 282
Carmel, NY 10512

Most reputable direct mail marketing services screen their mailing lists against the DMA's Mail Preference Service List. It costs direct mail marketers money to send an advertisement by mail, and thus it is beneficial to these marketers to remove from their mailing lists those persons who have expressed a clear desire not to receive such mailings. It makes no sense for a direct mail marketer to waste money sending advertising to someone who is simply going to throw it away without reading it. Most businesses update their direct mail marketing lists quarterly, so you should begin to see a noticeable decrease in junk mail reaching your mailbox within three months of sending your request.

## TELEMARKETING

You're just sitting down to dinner, or perhaps enjoying a quiet afternoon at home, and the telephone rings. "Hello Mrs. Jones . . . I am calling on behalf of the Fly-By-Night Company with a special offer; available today only. . . especially designed just for you . . . blah, blah, blah." Your peaceful afternoon or the enjoyment of your meal has just been interrupted by a telemarketer. Or has it? Although many people will tell any telemarketer calling their home to "take a hike" or to go somewhere else that's a bit hotter, there are still a significant number of people who will listen to a telemarketer's sales pitch and purchase whatever he is selling. From a personal privacy point of view you should *never* conduct any type of business with a telemarketer. Furthermore, when considering the threat of identity theft, telemarketing calls become a specific threat.

The problem we face from an identity theft point of view is that we really don't know who is on the other end of the telephone call. It could be a legitimate and reputable business marketing products over the telephone, or it could just as easily be a criminal trying to gain personal information about you for the purpose of identity theft. If you respond to a telemarketer's offer and decide to purchase whatever he is selling, you will be asked to provide a means of payment. You will normally provide a credit card number along with associated billing and identity information. If you have provided this information to a legitimate business, you will soon receive whatever it is you just ordered from the telemarketer. However, if you have just provided your personal identifying information, along with your credit card information, to an identity thief, you now have a very serious problem.

### DMA's Telephone Preference Service

As a first step toward protecting yourself from telemarketers, I recommend that you register with the DMA's Telephone

Preference Service. The DMA maintains a list of home telephone numbers of households that do not want to receive calls from telemarketers. All reputable national-level telemarketing companies screen their call lists against the DMA's Telephone Preference (Do Not Call) List to ensure that they are not placing calls to persons who object to telemarketing calls. Local businesses (e.g., your hometown newspaper), however, may not screen their call lists with the DMA when making calls in their area.

To register with the DMA Telephone Preference Service, send a written request to be added to the Do Not Call List to

**Direct Marketing Association**
Attn: Telephone Preference Service
P.O. Box 282
Carmel, NY 10512

This is a free service, and you will notice a marked reduction in telemarketing calls within a few months. You may also register with the Telephone Preference Service online at www.the-dma.org, but there is a $5 online service fee.

Once you've registered with the DMA Telephone Preference Service and given businesses time to update their Do Not Call Lists (usually about three months), you should no longer receive telemarketing calls. Should you receive a telemarketing call after registering, you can assume that the business placing the call is disreputable, irresponsible, some kind of scam, or the lead-in to identity theft.

When you register with the DMA Telephone Preference Service, you will remain on the Do Not Call List for five years.

## National Do Not Call Registry

The threat to personal privacy, the likelihood of telemarketing calls being high-pressure sales tactics or outright scams, and numerous consumer complaints about telemarketers finally led the federal government to create the National Do Not Call Registry.

The National Do Not Call Registry is a list of telephone numbers maintained in an FTC database of individuals/households that do not want to receive calls from telemarketers. Registration began in July 2003, and FTC enforcement of the Do Not Call Registry began that October. It works like this: Call the toll-free telephone number (1-888-382-1222) and follow the prompts. You will be asked to ensure that you are calling from the telephone number you wish to add to the Do Not Call Registry and to enter your telephone number on your telephone's Touch-Tone keypad. You may also register online on the Do Not Call Web site (www.donotcall.gov), where you can enter up to three telephone numbers at a time (perhaps you have two lines in your home and a cellular telephone). If you register online, you are also required to provide a valid e-mail address where a confirmation e-mail can be sent. When you receive the confirmation e-mail, just click on the included link and your telephone number(s) is added to the Do Not Call Registry. That's it. Once you have done this, telemarketers are prohibited from calling you with offers for their products or services. Your telephone number will remain in the National Do Not Call Registry for five years.

So will this stop 100 percent of telemarketing calls? Unfortunately, no. Businesses with which you have an established relationship (i.e., from which you have purchased a product or service in the past 18 months) or to which you have made an inquiry within the past three months may still contact you. Additionally, some businesses are exempt from the National Do Not Call Registry, including

- long-distance phone companies
- airlines
- banks and credit unions
- insurance businesses, to the extent that they are regulated by state law

However, while these specific businesses themselves may be exempt from the provisions of the National Do Not Call Registry, any *telemarketing companies they hire to conduct marketing on their behalf* must screen their calls against the registry and are prohibited from calling any number contained therein.

Telemarketers are required to update their Do Not Call Lists from the registry at least every three months. So from the time you register your telephone number with the National Do Not Call Registry, telemarketers have up to the full three months to add your telephone number to their Do Not Call Lists. Three months after you add your telephone number to the National Do Not Call Registry, it becomes unlawful for a telemarketer to call you, and said telemarketer may face a fine of up to $11,000 for doing so. If you receive a telemarketing call thereafter, you can file a complaint by accessing the Do Not Call Web site.

In October 2003 when the Do Not Call List became enforceable, there were more than 53 million households that had signed up with the National Do Not Call Registry expressing their desire to be left alone by telemarketers. The telemarketing industry immediately went to court and won injunctions to stop enforcement of the National Do Not Call Registry.

With amazing speed, Congress proposed and passed bills within just a couple days giving the FTC authority to enforce the National Do Not Call Registry. The House voted 412–8 and the Senate 95–0 in favor of the bill permitting enforcement of the registry. (Congress recognized the threat from telemarketers, and of course, 53 million potential voters got Congress to pay attention and act with some degree of speed.)

Finally, the 10th U.S. Circuit Court of Appeals blocked a lower court order barring the FTC from enforcing the registry of more than 53 million numbers. "The Supreme Court has held that there is undoubtedly a substantial governmental interest in the prevention of abusive and coercive sales practices," the ruling said.

If you have not already done so, add your telephone number to the National Do Not Call Registry.

## THE INTERNET

Does the use of the Internet increase the likelihood that you will become a victim of identity theft? If you shop online today, will you find numerous fraudulent charges on your credit card tomorrow? The short answer is no. The majority of identity theft occurs offline. Using the Internet and shopping online do not significantly increase the likelihood of your becoming a victim of identity theft.

It is important, however, to understand the risks associated with the Internet and how those risks relate to identity theft. Many online shoppers are concerned that in sending their personal information and credit card number over the Internet they are broadcasting this information to the world. Now, if you place this information *in an e-mail* and send it off to a company to make a purchase, you may in fact be broadcasting it. However, most companies that have a Web site and allow for online orders have set up a secure order system using Secure Socket Layer (SSL). SSL encrypts the information that travels across the Internet from your computer to that of the business with which you are doing your online shopping. Your Web browser will likely alert you when you access and leave a secure Web page. This is often indicated by the presence of a padlock on the task bar of your computer screen.

Although SSL secures your information in transit, it does not ensure that it is securely stored once it is received by the business receiving your order. Likewise, there is nothing to ensure that a business securely stores your order information if you provide it over the telephone or write it down and send it through the mail.

In general, shopping online with an established and reputable company using a Web site with SSL to transmit your orders is just as safe (if not more so) as placing an order over the telephone. Unfortunately, it can be difficult to tell if the Web site you are visiting and to which you are providing your personal and billing information is that of a legitimate business or that of an identity thief.

Of course, once you have identified the Web site of a reputable business from a trusted source, you should feel confident in using the online services provided by that business. However, as with cons and scams that occur in the physical world, you should be aware of those that occur online. It is important to recognize that when you are approached by a stranger offering you a "great deal" online, it may well be one of the many criminals who make their offers through unsolicited commercial e-mail, or spam.

The first and greatest threat on the Internet is spam. If you have an e-mail account, sooner or later you will begin to receive spam. Spam markets everything from drugs to child pornography to get-rich-quick schemes to home mortgages to fad diets and just about anything else you can think of. The one common thread running through these unsolicited commercial e-mail offers is that they are usually illegitimate. *Spam is a scam!*

Unfortunately, enough people fall for these scams and send off enough of their hard-earned money (for products and services they may never receive) to keep spammers in business. According to Brightmail, a San Francisco-based company specializing in the filtering and analysis of e-mail (as reported in the *Washington Times* on 1 August 2002), there were more than 4.8 million spam attacks in June 2002, up from 880,000 a year earlier. Mind you, the June 2002 figure does not represent 4.8 million pieces of unsolicited e-mail, but 4.8 million different attacks, each consisting of *thousands of pieces* of unsolicited e-mail!

According to Bryson Gordon, a product-line manager with the computer security company McAfee.Com, "Spam is transitioning from being a mere annoyance to a security threat." Gordon explains that spam poses a serious threat by capturing personal and private information through the use of false claims and misleading links. Spammers will establish a Web page and send out spam that mimics the advertising of a respected retail store, offering low sale prices on a number of different items to hundreds of thousands or millions of potential victims. Those who take the bait will follow links contained in the spam to a Web site that appears to be that of a respected store or business. Unfortunately for the victims of these scams, the Web pages are fakes and, according to Mr. Gordon, exist simply to capture people's credit card information.

To protect yourself from identity theft, it is very important that you never respond to spam. Even an e-mail that appears to be from a business you trust and have had good dealings with in the past may be a fake.

Now, this does not mean that you can't or shouldn't shop online. Online shopping allows you to compare products and prices from a wide variety of companies and choose the deal that best meets your needs and desires. As long as *you* are locating the companies with which you do business directly (for example, by using a search engine to search out the product you wish to buy), online shopping is perfectly OK.

On the other hand, if you discovered the company in question through spam, beware. Spam is a scam, and this may very well be a criminal's attempt to gather as many credit card numbers and as much associated billing information as possible.

As in the physical world, we need to remain cautious and aware of potential threats in cyberspace.

## COMPUTERS

Computers enable us to store and process massive amounts of information. The contents of a small library can be carried on a laptop computer. More importantly for those of us who use computers in our personal lives, they may contain all of our personal and financial information in one location—on the computer's hard drive.

We have already seen how information contained on computers can be lost or stolen. According to the Washington, DC, Metropolitan Police Department (http://mpdc.dc.gov/), "It is estimated that over 300,000 laptop computers were stolen in the U.S. in 1999 alone." Certainly, many of these were stolen simply for the value of the computers alone; a laptop is small, portable, and may cost as much as $5,000. However, it's safe to assume that much of the information contained on these stolen computers was used in the furtherance of other crimes.

If you keep personal information on your computer (e.g., budgets, account information, health/medical information, personal correspondence, and so on), you should store that information in a format that cannot be used by a thief should your computer be stolen. Simply put, this means storing your information in encrypted files. There are several top-quality encryption and security programs available to protect your computer files. I discuss a number of these that you can get for free in my book *Freeware Encryption and Security Programs: Protecting Your Computer and Your Privacy* (Paladin Press, 2001).

No matter what other type of computer security programs you choose to use to protect your personal information, I strongly encourage you to obtain a copy of PGP and incorporate it into your computer security planning. PGP is available free of charge for personal use and may be downloaded from various sources on the Internet. The best places to obtain the latest copy of PGP are from the Massachusetts Institute of Technology's PGP Distribution Site at http://web.mit.edu/network/pgp.html, the PGP International Site at www.pgpi.org, or from the PGP Corporation at www.pgp.com.

When encrypted using PGP, the previous sentence becomes totally unintelligible, as you can see in the following example:

——-BEGIN PGP MESSAGE——-
Version: PGP 8.0

qANQR1DDDQQJAwLq7R6fJflwA2DJwA9o
hnA5wGKGqn6n7W8I9krNpQSQ9cCcL8g1
cC2u8QIYBk8Fa+PNO4W+W37npbXiMQo

NnaJ9wBbhEdJjyaqbb2eaiW03Bi6aJ2e78SH
/PEmrx5auXbRPU5RCSeXjH2CYmvolw3/B
i0++RLRzk0d7eJKhUUPvOrfd2DTutKGX01
EltA6PtIQ4mAU1LrQuUGKxI2ihI0p4UnKyy
BV12gBZXuZElKnuzqN7UEh5/UJZs6UJjBfj
RtcT7pGAm3FYtK4z1WdCxVwSPXDTcSAt
5PVBR4s=
=hYPd

——-END PGP MESSAGE——-

By protecting the personal and private information stored on your computer, you can prevent the theft of your computer from turning into identity theft.

## YOUR SOCIAL SECURITY NUMBER— THE KEY TO IDENTITY THEFT

In order to steal your identity, a criminal needs to gather personal identifying information about you. While an identity thief will try to gather as much as possible, the one key piece of information he needs to make his crime successful is your Social Security number.

When Social Security numbers were introduced as part of the Social Security Act of 1935 there was a great deal of concern among the American people that such a numbering system could become a national ID number, thereby posing a significant threat to our rights and freedoms. It took little imagination on the part of our parents or grandparents in 1935 to envision the kind of harm that could be done by adopting a national identification number. National ID numbers were something those Nazis gaining power in Germany might do but never something that would be tolerated by free people in a constitutional republic.

In 1935 the American government agreed that a national ID number was certainly not something to be imposed on a free people and assured the nation that these new Social Security numbers would only be used to administer the Social Security program. Social Security cards were even printed with the annotation "NOT FOR IDENTIFICATION."

In 1943 President Franklin D. Roosevelt signed Executive Order 9397 that required federal agencies to use the Social Security number when creating new records and systems of records.

In the early 1960s the Internal Revenue Service (IRS) began using the Social Security number as a "taxpayer identification number," completely disregarding the government's original promises that the Social Security number would not be used for identification purposes.

On 1 October 2000, the government enacted a federal law, 42 U.S.C. Section 666(a)(13), under the pretext of enforcing child support laws. This law requires you to disclose your Social Security number in order to receive any type of government license, benefit, or recreational permit. Simply put, in order to obtain a driver's license, fishing license, marriage license, and so on, you must disclose your Social Security number, which is entered into the database of the issuing agency.

The federal government made the availability of welfare funds contingent upon states collecting Social Security numbers as part of its plan to enforce child support laws. Simply put, if a state or the people in general objected to disclosing their Social Security numbers, the federal government would cut off federal welfare funds used by the states to support the poor and the homeless.

To comply with the federal law, each state has passed laws requiring the collection of Social Security numbers on applications for professional and occupational licenses, commercial driver's licenses, recreational licenses, and marriage licenses. Additionally, in the Federal Balanced Budget Act of 1997 (taking effect 1 October 2000), the word "commercial" was deleted from the final version of the act, thereby requiring that Social Security numbers be collected for *all* driver's licenses, not just commercial licenses.

Strongly opposed by the states, this massive and unwarranted expansion of the Social Security number from a single-use account number into a national identification number served only to put us at risk of having our liberty, privacy, property, and lives violated by identity thieves and other criminals. In passing applicable state laws to comply with the federal mandate, many states complained that the federal government was using coercion to force the states to comply with this ill-conceived and dangerous requirement. Consider, for example, the comments recorded in Washington state law regarding the federally mandated use of Social Security numbers as a national identification number:

> The legislature declares that enhancing the effectiveness of child support enforcement is an essential public policy goal, but that the use of social security numbers on licenses is an inappropriate, intrusive, and offensive method of improving enforceability. The legislature also finds that, in 1997, the federal government threatened sanction by withholding of funds for programs for poor families if states did not comply with a federal requirement to use social security numbers on licenses, thus causing the legislature to enact such provisions under protest.
>
> (Revised Code of Washington RCW 26.23.150)

Despite this and similar protests by the states and their citizens, the federal mandate stood. Simply put, this means that unless you disclose your Social Security number to be entered into the databases of various state agencies, you will be denied your rightful liberties to travel the public highways (no driver's license), enjoy the natural resources and outdoors (no fishing license), even fall in love and get married (no marriage license). It has effectively become a national identification number.

Some may argue that while our Social Security numbers are certainly used far more than originally intended and promised by the government, they aren't national identification numbers.

After all, this isn't Communist China, nor is our government run like old Nazi Germany, requiring enumeration of all its citizens. The United States of America is a constitutional republic, a free nation of free people . . . we simply don't have national identification numbers. Yet, as abhorrent as national identification numbers should be to a free people, even the Social Security Administration admits that this is exactly what Social Security numbers *are.*

The testimony of James G. Huse Jr., inspector general of the Social Security Administration, regarding the Social Security Administration's response to the terrorist attack on 11 September 2001 stated,

> While never intended to be such, the SSN is used as our national identifier. . . . By acknowledging that the SSN is our virtual national identifier, we accept the responsibility to protect its integrity—not only to prevent the financial crimes that have historically defined SSN misuse, but to ensure that it is not used for other criminal purposes as well. A purloined SSN is as useful a tool for terrorists as it is for identity thieves. We must now address that reality as we continue our efforts to deal with these problems.

With the government using the Social Security number as a national identification number, the private sector quickly followed suit, requiring individuals to disclose their Social Security numbers as part of private transactions. Although purely private sector organizations have no legal authority to require you to disclose your Social Security number, the practice began with businesses that have government reporting requirements or are overseen by government regulators—such as banks and credit unions. With the various financial institutions now demanding that we disclose our Social Security numbers as a condition of doing business with them, related industries (e.g., insurance and medical) began demanding that we disclose our Social Security numbers. The major credit reporting agencies (the credit bureaus) use your Social Security number as a key to your credit reports, so now any business that may want to conduct a credit check on you demands your Social Security number. We have become so accustomed to disclosing our Social Security numbers that we even find them being demanded by businesses that have no legitimate use for them whatsoever (such as video rental stores).

Government and private industry are not blind to the significant threat we face as a result of having our Social Security numbers (and other personal identifying data) stored in every database from the federal government to the local video rental store. In fact, many of these agencies and businesses warn about the dangers of disclosing our Social Security numbers:

- Protect your Social Security number (SSN). Don't print it on your checks. Don't give it out unless it is required (on tax forms or employment records, for example). Be sure your driver's license uses an "assigned" number and not your SSN. SSNs are the key piece of information con artists most often use to commit "identity theft"—using your information to open accounts in your name and run up expenses.

  —Iowa Attorney General

- Be very careful about to whom you give out personal identification information such as your mother's maiden name and your Social Security number. Ask if it can be kept confidential. Inquire into how it will be used and with whom it will be shared. Social Security number: Give it out only when necessary. Ask to use other types of identifiers when possible. DO NOT store your Social Security card in your wallet.

  —New York Attorney General

- Don't pre-print your driver's license, telephone or Social Security numbers on your checks. Identity theft and account fraud happen when someone steals personal information such as your bank account number or Social Security number and then poses as you, either withdrawing money from your account or running up debt in your name, or both. The threat is real, and the government estimates 400,000 people are victimized by these crimes each year.

  —Chase Financial

- Be especially careful with sensitive personal information. Your Social Security number should not be requested except by an employer, government agency, lender, or credit bureau. If that information falls into the wrong hands, it can be used by someone to impersonate you in order to steal from your accounts or to steal from others in your name. Many states no longer use Social Security numbers on driver's licenses. Some states offer random numbers as alternatives and bar merchants from asking consumers to put their Social Security numbers on checks or credit card slips.

  —U.S. General Services Administration

- Identity theft occurs when someone gains access to another person's personal information, such as the DL number, Social Security number, bank or credit card account numbers, and uses them to commit fraud or theft. An impostor can use your identity to open fraudulent credit accounts, secure loans for cars and housing, or steal money from your bank accounts. Protect your Social Security number by not releasing it to anyone unless required by law.

  —California Department of Motor Vehicles

- Your Social Security number is the most valuable piece of your personal financial information because it is your main identifying number for employment, tax reporting, and credit history tracking purposes. If your Social Security number falls in the hands of a thief, you could face serious problems as a result. A thief could use your Social Security number to obtain employment, open credit card accounts, or obtain loans under your name. The best way to protect yourself is to guard your Social Security number and provide it to others only when absolutely necessary.

  —New York Better Business Bureau

- By revealing our SSNs to so many entities—governmental and private organizations alike—we're sacrificing our right to privacy and anonymity. And in an information society, these are increasingly rare commodities. But because the SSN is so commonly used as an individual account number, this nine-digit code ends up being a virtual pass key to a vast amount of private, and often sensitive, information about you—your address, medical history, shopping preferences, household income, and use of prescription drugs, to name just a few. Use caution when giving out your SSN to a government agency. They are required by the Privacy Act of 1974 to tell you why your SSN is necessary, whether giving your SSN is mandatory or voluntary, and how your SSN will be used. And stop giving your SSN to private organizations. Suggest they use an alternative identifying number. If they refuse, think about taking your business elsewhere. They'll get the hint.

  —American Civil Liberties Union (ACLU)

- ID theft puts an ugly face on your good name. A con

artist who knows your Social Security number, bank account information, or other personal details can temporarily become you in order to commit fraud. Fixing the damage could take years. Social Security numbers (SSNs) are especially hot items for identity thieves because they often are the key to getting new credit cards, applying for federal benefit payments, or opening other doors to money. The Social Security Administration says that consumer complaints about the alleged misuse of SSNs are rising dramatically, from about 8,000 in 1997 to more than 30,000 in 1999. "Giving your number is voluntary, even when you are asked for the number directly," says the Social Security Administration. "If requested, you should ask why your number is needed, how your number will be used, what law requires you to give your number, and what the consequences are if you refuse."

—Federal Deposit Insurance Corporation (FDIC)

- Don't carry your Social Security number; leave it in a secure place. Give your SSN only when absolutely necessary. Ask to use other types of identifiers when possible. Before revealing any personal information, find out how it will be used and whether it will be shared with others.

  —U.S. Postal Service (USPS)

- Social Security numbers are the key to much of the financial, medical, and other personal information that most people would like to keep confidential. Yet the numbers are so widely used, by business and government, that they have acquired a special status as a security risk.

  —California Office of Privacy Protection

- Don't include information such as your driver's license or Social Security numbers on your pre-printed checks.

  —Washington Mutual Bank

- Do not write your personal identification number (PIN), Social Security number, or credit card account number on checks or on your ATM or debit card. Provide your Social Security number only when necessary.

  —State Farm Insurance Corporation

- Protect your Social Security number. Limit its use as identification; and never preprint your driver's license or Social Security number on your checks.

  —First Charter Financial Services of North Carolina

- Today the Social Security number has become the key to detailed government portraiture of our private lives. Even the Secretary of Health and Human Services (HHS) now describes American Social Security numbers as a "de facto personal identifier." Kristin Davis, senior associate editor for *Kiplinger's Personal Finance Magazine*, recently described the growing use of social security numbers as an all-purpose ID as the "single biggest threat to protecting our financial identities."

  —Charlotte Twight, Ph.D., J.D. (professor and privacy expert, Boise State University, before a hearing of the Subcommittee on Government Management, Information, and Technology, 18 May 2000)

- U.S. PIRG believes that the widespread availability of the Social Security number contributes to identity theft, which is well documented as one of the nation's fastest growing white-collar crimes.

—U.S. Public Interest Research Group (before the Subcommittee on Social Security House Ways and Means Committee Hearing on Misuse of Social Security Numbers, 22 May 2001)

- Beware of anyone asking for your Social Security number. If they refuse to complete a transaction without it, consider taking your business elsewhere.

  —Nolo Law For All (Identity Theft FAQ)

- The crime of identity theft is increasing at epidemic proportions. With the Social Security number accessible to so many people, it is relatively easy for someone to fraudulently use your SSN to assume your identity and gain access to your bank account, credit accounts, utilities records, and other sources of personal information. . . . Adopt an active policy of not giving out your SSN unless you are convinced it is required or is to your benefit. Make people show you why it is needed.

  —Privacy Rights Clearinghouse, Fact Sheet # 10

## The Social Security Number in Canada Is a SIN

The threat from the issuance and misuse of a national identification number is not unique to the United States. In Canada the Social Security number is known as the Social Insurance number, or SIN. Our Canadian neighbors are suffering from the same misuse of their SIN that we in the United States are from that of our SSN.

In 1998 the office of the auditor general of Canada conducted a review of the management of the Canadian Social Insurance number and found many problems, just a few of which are highlighted here:

- The role of the Social Insurance number has expanded gradually.
- The SIN has become a de facto national identifier for income-related transactions, contrary to the government's intent.
- There is a significant gap between number of living SIN holders and size of the Canadian population. Valid SINs are held by thousands of individuals with no legal status in Canada.
- Minimal effort is dedicated to SIN investigations.
- Unregulated use of SIN in the private sector is a key vulnerability.

Four years later the office of the auditor general of Canada reviewed its findings and stated, "In 2002 we returned, expecting to find that the problems reported in 1998 would have been largely resolved. Instead, we found that progress on some key issues has been limited. The continuing weakness in the issuing of SINs leads us to conclude that HRDC has not done enough to safeguard and strengthen the integrity of the SIN." (HRDC is Human Resources Development Canada, the Canadian government agency responsible for the SIN.)

## Your Last Four

A very common practice regarding requests for Social Security number information is to ask that you disclose the last four digits only. The rationale is that this partial disclosure somehow safeguards you from possible compromise of your Social Security number. Unfortunately, disclosing "your last four" does nothing to protect you, and it may be the exact information an identity thief is looking for.

Many businesses are taking steps to limit disclosure of individuals' Social Security numbers contained in their databases by masking portions of the number. In reviewing credit report header information, I saw that Social Security numbers were masked in this manner: SSN: 123-45-XXXX. Yes, they masked the last four digits of the Social Security number. Now, credit report header information (as opposed to the complete credit report) is generally available to anyone who wishes to obtain it. So an identity thief obtaining a copy of your credit report header information has all but the last four digits of your Social Security number.

But credit header information isn't the only place one's Social Security number can be found. I contacted an online database called Alumni Finder (www.alumnifinder.com) after learning that they would disclose personal information containing Social Security numbers to their subscribers. What I discovered is that Alumni Finder is part of Market Models, Inc., of Wickford, Rhode Island. Market Models is a mass-marketing company using data specialists to provide potential customer lists with "several layers of key marketing data," including such information as names, mailing information, fax numbers, domain names, and phone numbers. In obtaining my own personal information from Alumni Finder/Market Models, Inc., I found that its database also apparently includes Social Security numbers, although they took steps to protect the disclosure of my Social Security number by masking the last four digits, listing it in the format 123-45-XXXX.

To be fair, these marketing companies and other related businesses are at least making some effort to shield disclosure of Social Security numbers contained in their databases. They recognize the extensive harm that can be done should an identity thief gain access to someone's Social Security number and associated information in their databases. The problem, however, is that there is no consistency in the way the Social Security numbers are protected from one company to the next. Some mask the last four numbers, others disclose only the last four numbers, and others disclose the last five numbers. Because of this, you should never feel safe disclosing any portion of your Social Security number whatsoever.

By disclosing the last four digits of your Social Security number, you may be giving an identity thief the last bit of information he needs to steal your identity. It is important to understand that every time you disclose your Social Security number, in whole or in part, you are putting yourself at risk. The next time someone asks for the last four digits of your Social Security number, *just say NO!*

The numerous warnings above (and many more like them found in the privacy and security policies of various corporations and government agencies) should make it obvious that disclosure of your Social Security number is a very bad idea, always putting you at risk of becoming a victim of identity theft or other crimes.

Along this same line, any business that continues to use your Social Security number as a key to your identity or as an account number or password is operating with gross negligence, showing a complete disregard for your safety, and acting with total irresponsibility with regard to the security of the records it maintains about you. If any business requests your Social Security number, ask that business to cite the specific law that requires you to provide it and ask specifically why it's needed. If there is no law that requires a business to collect your SSN and that business still asks for it, take your business elsewhere and make public the irresponsible conduct of the business involved. They'll get the message.

## Identity Theft Prevention Act of 2003

The only way to truly fix the problem caused by the widespread misuse of Social Security numbers is to pass a law that restricts their use to Social Security purposes only and prohibits the establishment of a similar national identification number in the future.

A bill currently before Congress that would accomplish this is the Identity Theft Prevention Act of 2003, introduced by Congressman Ron Paul (R-Texas). If we hope to stop the ever-growing crime of identity theft and threats to our personal privacy, it will be necessary to pass this or a very similar bill into law very soon. The Identity Theft Prevention Act of 2003 is short and to the point and is provided here for your reference:

108th CONGRESS
1st Session
**H. R. 220**

To amend title II of the Social Security Act and the Internal Revenue Code of 1986 to protect the integrity and confidentiality of Social Security account numbers issued under such title, to prohibit the establishment in the Federal Government of any uniform national identifying number, and to prohibit Federal agencies from imposing standards for identification of individuals on other agencies or persons.

**IN THE HOUSE OF REPRESENTATIVES**

**January 7, 2003**

Mr. PAUL (for himself, Mr. BARTLETT of Maryland, and Mr. HINCHEY) introduced the following bill; which was referred to the Committee on Ways and Means, and in addition to the Committee on Government Reform, for a period to be subsequently determined by the Speaker, in each case for consideration of such provisions as fall within the jurisdiction of the committee concerned

**A BILL**

To amend title II of the Social Security Act and the Internal Revenue Code of 1986 to protect the integrity and confidentiality of Social Security account numbers issued under such title, to prohibit the establishment in the Federal Government of any uniform national identifying number, and to prohibit Federal agencies from imposing standards for identification of individuals on other agencies or persons.

*Be it enacted by the Senate and House of Representatives of the United States of America in Congress assembled,*

**SECTION 1. SHORT TITLE.**

This Act may be cited as the 'Identity Theft Prevention Act of 2003.'

**SEC. 2. RESTRICTIONS ON THE USE OF THE SOCIAL SECURITY ACCOUNT NUMBER.**

(a) REPEAL OF PROVISIONS AUTHORIZING CERTAIN USAGES OF THE SOCIAL SECURITY ACCOUNT NUMBER- Section 205(c)(2) of the Social Security Act (42 U.S.C. 405(c)(2)) is amended—

(1) in subparagraph (C), by striking '(C)(i) It is the policy' and all that follows through clause (vi);

(2) by striking subparagraphs (C)(ix), (E), and (H); and

(3) by redesignating subparagraphs (F) and (G) as subparagraphs (E) and (F), respectively.

(b) NEW RULES APPLICABLE TO SOCIAL SECURITY ACCOUNT NUMBERS- Section 205(c)(2) of such Act is amended further—

(1) by inserting after subparagraph (B) the following:

'(C)(i) All social security account numbers issued under this subsection shall be randomly generated.

'(ii) Except as otherwise provided in this paragraph–

'(I) the socal security account number issued under this subsection to any individual shall be the exclusive property of such individual, and

'(II) the Social Security Administration shall not divulge the social security account number issued to any individual under this subsection to any agency or instrumentality of the Federal Government, to any

State, political subdivision of a State, or agency or instrumentality of a State or political subdivision thereof, or to any other individual.

'(iii) Clause (ii) shall not apply with respect to the use of the social security account number as an identifying number to the extent provided in section 6109(d) of the Internal Revenue Code of 1986 (relating to use of the social security account number for social security and related purposes).'; and

(2) by redesignating clauses (vii) and (viii) of subparagraph (C) as clauses (iv) and (v), respectively.

(c) USE OF SOCIAL SECURITY ACCOUNT NUMBERS UNDER INTERNAL REVENUE CODE- Subsection (d) of section 6109 of the Internal Revenue Code of 1986 is amended—

(1) in the heading, by inserting 'FOR SOCIAL SECURITY AND RELATED PURPOSES' after 'NUMBER'; and

(2) by striking 'this title' and inserting 'section 86, chapter 2, and subtitle C of this title.'

(d) EFFECTIVE DATES AND RELATED RULES-

(1) EFFECTIVE DATES- Not later than 60 days after the date of the enactment of this Act, the Commissioner of Social Security shall publish in the Federal Register the date determined by the Commissioner, in consultation with the Secretary of the Treasury, to be the earliest date thereafter by which implementation of the amendments made by this section is practicable. The amendments made by subsection (a) shall take effect on the earlier of such date or the date which occurs 5 years after the date of the enactment of this Act. The amendments made by subsection (b) shall apply with respect to social security account numbers issued on or after such earlier date. The amendments made by subsection (c)

shall apply with respect to calendar quarters and taxable years beginning on or after such earlier date.
(2) REISSUANCE OF NUMBERS— The Commissioner of Social Security shall ensure that, not later than 5 years after the date of the enactment of this Act, all individuals who have been issued social security account numbers under section 205(c) of the Social Security Act as of the date prior to the earlier date specified in paragraph (1) are issued new social security account numbers in accordance with such section as amended by this section. Upon issuance of such new social security account numbers, any social security account numbers issued to such individuals prior to such earlier date specified in paragraph (1) shall be null and void and subject to the requirements of section 205(c)(2)(C)(ii)(II) of such Act, as amended by this section. Nothing in this section or the amendments made thereby shall be construed to preclude the Social Security Administration and the Secretary of the Treasury from cross-referencing such social security account numbers newly issued to individuals pursuant to this paragraph to the former social security account numbers of such individuals for purposes of administering title II or title XVI of such Act or administering the Internal Revenue Code of 1986 in connection with section 86, chapter 2, and subtitle C thereof.

## SEC. 3. CONFORMING AMENDMENTS TO THE PRIVACY ACT OF 1974.

(a) IN GENERAL- Section 7 of the Privacy Act of 1974 (5 U.S.C. 552a note, 88 Stat. 1909) is amended–

(1) in subsection (a), by striking paragraph (2) and inserting the following:

'(2) The provisions of paragraph (1) of this subsection

shall not apply with respect to any disclosure which is required under regulations of the commissioner of social security pursuant to section 205(c)(2) of the social security act or under regulations of the secretary of the treasury pursuant to section 6109(d) of the internal revenue code of 1986.'; and

(2) by striking subsection (b) and inserting the following:

'(b) Except with respect to disclosures described in subsection (a)(2), no agency or instrumentality of the Federal Government, a State, a political subdivision of a State, or any combination of the foregoing may request an individual to disclose his social security account number, on either a mandatory or voluntary basis.'.

(b) EFFECTIVE DATE- The amendments made by this section shall take effect on the earlier date specified in section 2(d)(1).

**SEC. 4. PROHIBITION OF GOVERNMENT-WIDE UNIFORM IDENTIFYING NUMBERS.**

(a) IN GENERAL- Except as authorized under section 205(c)(2) of the Social Security Act, any two agencies or instrumentalities of the Federal Government may not implement the same identifying number with respect to any individual.

(b) IDENTIFYING NUMBERS- For purposes of this section—

(1) the term 'identifying number' with respect to an individual means any combination of alpha-numeric symbols which serves to identify such individual, and

(2) any identifying number and any one or more derivatives of such number shall be treated as the same identifying number.

(c) EFFECTIVE DATE- The provisions of this section shall take effect January 1, 2005.

## SEC. 5. PROHIBITION OF GOVERNMENT-ESTABLISHED IDENTIFIERS.

(a) IN GENERAL- Subject to subsection (b), a Federal agency may not—

(1) establish or mandate a uniform standard for identification of an individual that is required to be used by any other Federal agency, a State agency, or a private person for any purpose other than the purpose of conducting the authorized activities of the Federal agency establishing or mandating the standard; or

(2) condition receipt of any Federal grant or contract or other Federal funding on the adoption, by a State, a State agency, or a political subdivision of a State, of a uniform standard for identification of an individual.

(b) TRANSACTIONS BETWEEN PRIVATE PERSONS- Notwithstanding subsection (a), a Federal agency may not establish or mandate a uniform standard for identification of an individual that is required to be used within the agency, or by any other Federal agency, a State agency, or a private person, for the purpose of—

(1) investigating, monitoring, overseeing, or otherwise regulating a transaction to which the Federal Government is not a party; or

(2) administrative simplification.

(c) REPEALER- Any provision of Federal law enacted before, on, or after the date of the enactment of this Act that is inconsistent with subsection (a) or (b) is repealed, including sections 1173(b) and 1177(a)(1) of the Social Security Act (42 U.S.C. 1320d-2(b); 42 U.S.C. 1320d-6(a)(1)).

(d) DEFINITIONS- For purposes of this section:

(1) AGENCY- The term 'agency' means any of the following:

(A) An Executive agency (as defined in section 105 of title 5, United States Code).
(B) A military department (as defined in section 102 of such title).
(C) An agency in the executive branch of a State government.
(D) An agency in the legislative branch of the Government of the United States or a State government.
(E) An agency in the judicial branch of the Government of the United States or a State government.

(2) STATE- The term 'State' means any of the several States, the District of Columbia, the Virgin Islands, the Commonwealth of Puerto Rico, Guam, American Samoa, the Commonwealth of the Northern Mariana Islands, the Republic of the Marshall Islands, the Federated States of Micronesia, or the Republic of Palau.

(e) EFFECTIVE DATE- The provisions of this section shall take effect January 1, 2005.

As you can see, the Identity Theft Prevention Act of 2003 would eliminate the widespread misuse of Social Security numbers by returning the Social Security number to its original purpose of managing our Social Security accounts. This is exactly what the government promised when it first established Social Security numbers anyway.

Despite the tremendous amount of good and the major benefit that would come from passing the Identity Theft Prevention Act of 2003 into law, there is, unfortunately, some opposition to this bill. This opposition is almost entirely from uncaring government bureaucrats and representatives of big business who use Social Security numbers for tracking and accounting purposes. They point out that passage of this bill would require them to assign new account numbers, which would entail additional work on the part of their agency or business. While this may be true, the advantages of preventing identity theft and the billions of dollars in annual loss from this crime far outweigh any additional cost or work that might be associated with using our Social Security numbers only for the purpose for which they were originally established.

## FALSE DRIVER'S LICENSES AND IDENTITY DOCUMENTS

For much of the identity thief's criminal activity, photo ID is necessary. When he wants to cash a check (or make a purchase using a personal check), he will likely be asked for photo ID. He will need a photo ID in order to open accounts at a bank. He will certainly be asked for photo ID when applying for a loan.

Unfortunately, the people asking him for photo ID are almost never qualified as document examiners. The local bartender is probably much more adept than the local bank teller at spotting a fake ID. The bartender expects a number of underage kids to attempt to get him to serve them a drink throughout the year. The kid trying to buy beer with a fake ID is so common that it has become a cliché. However, the 40-year-old woman opening an account at the local bank is seldom thought of as likely to be in possession of a fake ID.

It is fairly easy to obtain a passable fake ID through the mail and even easier, using your home computer and a high-quality printer, to produce fake ID that will fool almost anyone. Although I have no direct association with any of the following companies, they may serve as examples of places where one could purchase a good-quality fake ID.

- www.phonyid.com—This company, located in Sweden, produces a high-quality ID that bears a very close resemblance to U.S. driver's licenses.
- www.novelty-ids.com—This company produces a very believable ID. Although the ID cards do not copy

the appearance of actual state driver's licenses and identification cards, they would easily pass inspection unless the person doing the checking has an ID checking guide or knows what a specific state's driver's license is supposed to look like.

- www.qualityids.com—This company, located in Germany, provides a high-quality ID that is a close match to the driver's licenses issued by each of the 50 states, as well as Social Security cards and secondary ID cards.

There are many other companies that sell fake/novelty ID cards and supporting documentation. Searching the Internet with terms like "fake ID" and "novelty ID" will provide you with hundreds of links. Of course, many of these sites offer products that are little better than useless as part of an identity theft scam, but as we have seen, there are other sites that offer ID and products that are highly effective.

If you have a home computer and a good printer, it is also possible to produce quality fake ID right at home. There are several books available that take you step-by-step through the process. In 1996 Ragnar Benson wrote the book *Acquiring New ID: How to Easily Use the Latest Computer Technology to Drop Out, Start Over, and Get On with Your Life* (Paladin Press), a step-by-step guide to producing fake ID at home. Five years later, Sheldon Charrett, having seen the advances in computer and printing technology, wrote *Secrets of a Back-Alley ID Man: Fake ID Construction Techniques of the Underground* (Paladin Press). These books and many others like them provide detailed instruction on producing ID that will pass all but the most detailed inspection.

It is not my intent here to give detailed instructions on the construction of fake ID but rather to point out the ease with which an identity thief can produce a fake ID in your name once he obtains your personal identity information. I will, however, provide a brief overview of how construction of a fake ID might be accomplished.

First, the thief will need to get a template for your fake ID. This is not a major problem, since the designs of all state ID cards and driver's licenses are published in books like *ID Checking Guide* (www.driverslicenseguide.com). The advertising for this guide promises "*Every valid driver's license format shown in actual size and full color, so no 'con artist' can fool you (all 50 states and 10 Canadian provinces, too.)*" The *ID Checking Guide* is a very useful tool for comparing the format of state-issued ID cards and driver's licenses with something being presented as an issued ID. It is also exactly what the identity thief needs to scan ID formats into his home computer for the purpose of creating fake ID. It is especially interesting to note that if someone uses the *ID Checking Guide* to check an ID made by scanning a format from the *ID Checking Guide* itself, the scanned version will be a very good match.

After scanning the template into the computer, the identity thief fills in the blanks on the ID card with your personal identifying information. The addition of a passport-type or digital photo of the identity thief links his face with your identity. A few finishing touches, such as holograms, lamination, and authorizing signatures, and the identity thief has an ID in your name.

I have tried the techniques for making fake ID detailed in the above-listed books and was able to produce a convincing ID in an hour or two. The fakes were not perfect by any means, but they were certainly good enough to cash your checks or open accounts in your name.

Remember, people tend to believe what they see. Unless there is a good reason to question what we are being shown and told, we tend to accept things at face value. When an identity thief presents fake ID, the person checking that ID will most likely accept it as valid. The trick, of course, is not to give that person a good reason to question what he is being shown. If the ID presented appears to be professionally produced and there are no obvious errors, such as misspellings, ink smudges, or a blatant mismatch to the person presenting it (e.g., a 22-year-old white woman presenting the ID of a 65-year-old black man), it will almost always be accepted.

If someone were to attempt to verify the ID presented, it is very likely that the validity would be confirmed. Remember, the identity thief has not simply made up information to fill in the blanks of his fake ID—he has filled in the blanks with *your* personal identifying information. If you call your state department of motor vehicles (DMV) to verify the validity of a driver's license, you will be asked to provide the driver's license number, the name on the license, and perhaps the date of birth from the license. The DMV will then confirm that this information matches what is in its database.

The police might not even question the validity of a license that comes back verified when they run it through their computer system. While writing this book, I spoke with a couple of patrol officers from the state police and asked them if they are generally on the lookout for fake ID during their official contacts with people (e.g., during traffic stops). The officers explained that while they are certainly aware of the possibility of being presented with fake ID, it is not something that is on the top of their list to check during a contact. Many perfectly valid licenses are not in great condition anyway after they have been carried around in a wallet or pocket for a couple of years. Furthermore, police officers are not necessarily any more aware of the design and format of a license from another state than you or I are. Both police officers confirmed that as long as their contact was the result of a minor traffic infraction or some petty offense, and the computer verified what was being presented on the license (the fake ID), they probably wouldn't question its validity. Again, people will generally believe what they see and hear unless given a specific reason to believe it is false.

It is essential that you safeguard your personal information, or it may end up on the fake ID of an identity thief.

# 3

# Credit Bureaus, Private Investigators, and Information Brokers

*"Possibly the most systematic security threat to American consumers is 'identity theft,' which usually involves insider abuse of credit bureau databases."*

—News from the Office of the Privacy Commissioner (New Zealand)
Issue No. 21, January 1998

The major credit bureaus, or credit reporting agencies, gather extensive information about the financial activities of millions of individuals. The stated purpose of this is to provide credit grantors with a means of determining, on the basis of credit history, the creditworthiness of anyone applying for credit. This is a fairly reasonable concept—helping credit grantors avoid losses by enabling them to extend major lines of credit to only those individuals who have shown that they pay their debts in a timely manner.

The credit bureaus gather financial information about you from many sources, including banks, credit unions, and credit card companies. These types of businesses, known as automatic subscribers, report to the credit bureaus on a monthly basis regarding your payment history. In return, these subscribers can obtain reports from the credit bureaus at a discount. In addition, utility companies, medical facilities, insurance companies, and many other businesses that extend any type of credit or financing report information to the credit bureaus. These businesses may not report regular payment histories; rather, they only file reports when payments are severely overdue, collection action has been taken, or the debt is written off as bad or uncollectible. The credit bureaus also obtain information from public records, such as bankruptcies, tax liens, garnishments, and various other court orders and judgments. The compilation of these reports and records into specific files about individuals provides a fairly extensive (if not always accurate) overview of their financial habits.

One problem with credit bureau reporting is that it is often inaccurate. An 18 December 2002 CBSNews.com report stated, "A study by advocacy groups suggest that many [credit reports] have errors or omissions that can hurt your chances of getting a good interest rate on a loan. . . . More than a third of consumers could be hurt by the discrepancies, the groups claim." With the credit reporting agencies adding hundreds of thousands of new pieces of information to their databases every month, it is inevitable that errors and omissions will occur. Unfortunately, the credit reporting agencies make no significant effort to prevent or correct these errors (if they did, a third of their records would not contain discrepancies). Furthermore, the lack of screening of credit reports for accuracy is what enables many things that an identity thief does to go unnoticed and uncorrected until a consumer's credit rating has incurred significant damage.

An additional concern is the unauthorized dissemination of

information from your credit reports. This problem arises when the credit bureaus release information that is used for purposes other than establishing your creditworthiness to potential credit grantors with whom you have initiated a transaction. The credit bureaus have found that their databases, containing private financial information about millions of individuals, are a valuable commodity in and of themselves. They sell information about the creditworthiness of consumers to private investigators, information brokers, companies doing financial prescreening for marketing purposes, government agencies, and many others.

The credit bureaus are private companies seeking to make a profit. This means that they will sell information about you to anyone who has a permissible use for that information, as defined by the Fair Credit Reporting Act (Section 604):

### § 604. Permissible purposes of reports

(a) IN GENERAL.–Subject to subsection (c), any consumer reporting agency may furnish a consumer report under the following circumstances and no other:

(1) In response to the order of a court having jurisdiction to issue such an order, or a subpoena issued in connection with proceedings before a Federal grand jury.

(2) In accordance with the written instructions of the consumer to whom it relates. {{2-28-03 p. 6605}}

(3) To a person which it has reason to believe–

(A) intends to use the information in connection with a credit transaction involving the consumer on whom the information is to be furnished and involving the extension of credit to, or review or collection of an account of, the consumer; or

(B) intends to use the information for

employment purposes; or

(C) intends to use the information in connection with the underwriting of insurance involving the consumer; or

(D) intends to use the information in connection with a determination of the consumer's eligibility for a license or other benefit granted by a governmental instrumentality required by law to consider an applicant's financial responsibility or status; or

(E) intends to use the information, as a potential investor or servicer, or current insurer, in connection with a valuation of, or an assessment of the credit or prepayment risks associated with, an existing credit obligation; or

(F) otherwise has a legitimate business need for the information–

(i) in connection with a business transaction that is initiated by the consumer; or

(ii) to review an account to determine whether the consumer continues to meet the terms of the account.

(4) In response to a request by the head of a State or local child support enforcement agency (or a State or local government official authorized by the head of such an agency), if the person making the request certifies to the consumer reporting agency that–

(A) the consumer report is needed for the purpose of establishing an individual's capacity to make child support payments or determining the appropriate level of such payments;

> (B) the paternity of the consumer for the child to which the obligation relates has been established or acknowledged by the consumer in accordance with State laws under which the obligation arises (if required by those laws);
> (C) the person has provided at least 10 days' prior notice to the consumer whose report is requested, by certified or registered mail to the last known address of the consumer, that the report will be requested; and
> (D) the consumer report will be kept confidential, will be used solely for a purpose described in subparagraph (A), and will not be used in connection with any other civil, administrative, or criminal proceeding, or for any other purpose.

In addition to being collected by the credit bureaus, your personal information is also sought by private investigators and information brokers.

Private investigators range from individuals with little or no training to some of the very best qualified investigators in the world. Along this same line, private investigators have codes of conduct and ethical standards ranging from none at all to some of the highest professional ethics you will find in any business. Unfortunately, highly skilled does not always mean highly ethical. It takes little effort to find stories of private investigators conducting investigations for and providing information to individuals who used that information for criminal purposes. Even when private investigators and information brokers run legitimate businesses and provide a valuable service to the public (which most in fact do), they have very little control over how the information they provide is actually used.

An extreme example of the misuse of information provided

by these investigators can be found in the case of the murder of Rebecca Schaeffer, the star of the TV series *My Sister Sam*. A fan infatuated with Schaeffer hired a private investigator to obtain personal identifying information about her. The fan (Robert Bardo) obtained Schaeffer's home address from the private investigator and in July 1989 went to her home and shot her to death.

In a very similar case, Amy Boyer was murdered by Liam Youens, who used the services of information broker DocuSearch to obtain Boyer's Social Security number. He then used the services of a private investigator, who made a pretext call to Boyer, posing as a representative of her insurance company who needed to confirm her employment information. Boyer, believing that she was dealing with a representative of her insurance company, provided details of her employment, including her work location. This information was sold to Liam Youens, who then used it to locate Boyer and murder her.

Admittedly, the use of private investigators and information brokers to obtain information about an individual and thereafter use it to plan that person's murder is an extreme (although not particularly rare) example. However, the information provided by private investigators and information brokers can also be used to commit the crime of identity theft. An information broker gathers data from public and nonpublic records, compiling that information into searchable databases and selling reports from those databases to various clients. An information broker may work with national and international systems of records or may focus on a specific state or region.

I know an investigator/information broker who makes a particular effort to collect information from various state and local public, semipublic, and private records and compile it into extensive databases. Using database linking and analysis software, she is able to discover extensive background information about individuals, determine associations, and predict possibilities with uncanny accuracy. She of course has the standard databases of telephone directories, tax rolls, voter registration lists, and similar public records, but she also obtains information that might be considered only semipublic or even private. For example, current federal law mandates that in order to obtain any type of government license or benefit one must disclose one's Social Security number to the agency providing that license or benefit (including state agencies). This includes such things as marriage licenses. Applications for a marriage license in the state where this investigator works now require that both parties to the license include their Social Security numbers on the application. The state involved here doesn't print the Social Security numbers on the marriage license itself, but the applications are filed in the state archives, where they are accessible to my friend the investigator (and pretty much anyone else who knows what to ask for). The state is mandating the disclosure of what is clearly personal and private information and then filing this information where it may be accessed by the general public!

Along this same line, consider voter registration records—which by their very nature should be public. Voter registration information contains not only the names and addresses of registered voters but may contain private information such as unlisted telephone numbers or even the key to identity theft, Social Security numbers. (Social Security numbers were required on voter registration records in Virginia until the 4th U.S. Circuit Court struck the policy down.)

The investigator I mention here works in only two states and limits her collection of information to the states in which she works. There are, however, major companies that gather public, semipublic, and private information on a national basis, store it in databases, and sell it in reports to their clients.

The major information brokers in the United States are members of the Individual Reference Services Group (IRSG) (www.irsg.org). These few private corporations (along with the three major credit bureaus) gather personal data about millions of Americans and then use that information as a commodity that they buy, sell, and trade in the name of corporate profit. (It should be noted that while the following individual companies are all currently in business, the IRSG may be phased out because of passage of the Financial Services Modernization Act, or Gramm-Leach-Bliley Act, and other recent legislation.)

**Acxiom Corporation**
301 Industrial Blvd., HQB2
Conway, AR 72033

**ChoicePoint, Inc.**
1000 Alderman Dr.
Alpharetta, GA 30005

**DCS Information Systems**
500 North Central
Suite 280
Plano, TX 75074

**Dolan Media Company**
1650 Park Building
650 3rd Avenue South
Minneapolis, MN 55402

**First Data Solutions Inc.**
10825 Old Mill Road
Omaha, NE 68154

**LEXIS-NEXIS**
1150 18th Street, NW
Suite 600
Washington, DC 20036

**LocatePlus.com**
100 Cummings Center, Suite 235M
Beverly, MA 01915

**Online Professional**
**Electronic Network (OPEN)**
1650 Lake Shore Dr., Suite 350
Columbus, OH 43204

**Stanton Corp. dba Pinkerton Services Group, Inc.**
13950 Ballantyne Corporate Place
Suite 300
Charlotte, NC 28277-2712

**United Reporting Publishing Corp.**
P.O. Box 1967
Rancho Cordova, CA 95741-1967

**US Search.com Inc.**
5401 Beethoven St.
Los Angeles, CA 90066

**West Group**
610 Opperman Dr.
Eagan, MN 55123

One of the major problems created by these information brokers' gathering and selling of information on a nationwide basis is that it can provide an identity thief with information to which he would otherwise not be able to gain access. The brokers claim that they are only providing information available from public records, that the identity thief could gather such information himself, or that they are only providing information obtained from third-party providers. While this may be technically true, information brokers make it much easier for criminals to access this type of information.

It's important to understand that even (or especially) information contained in public records can help an identity thief gain access to your accounts and assume your identity. For example, many banks and other companies that establish accounts for customers will ask that you provide your mother's maiden name as a way for them to confirm your identity later if you make inquiries about your account. Remember, they are not using your mother's maiden name to confirm your identity at the time you establish the account but will use it as a future check (like a password) should you call with an inquiry about the account at some later date. The problem with this is that your mother's maiden name is contained in public records. Your mother's maiden name is on *your* birth certificate, and birth certificates are public record.

In many cases private information contained in public records (e.g., marriage license applications, voter registration cards, driver's licenses) is put there voluntarily by individuals (who may not know that it can be omitted). In other cases, as with Social Security numbers, it may be mandated. When companies gather records from across the nation and compile them into databases, thereafter selling reports from these databases, they make the work of an identity thief that much easier. I certainly do not want to imply that these investigators and information brokers are doing anything illegal. They are providing a service and acting within the letter of the law. (The best of these companies will even allow you to opt out of their reporting of private information.) Nonetheless, the lack of extensive security procedures to ensure accuracy and restrict access to these databases poses a very real threat to those whose names are contained therein.

I believe *any company* that gathers, compiles, or sells personal and private information should allow *anyone* identified in its records to opt out of the sharing of his or her nonpublic data, and furthermore should restrict access to its accumulated public records—or *at least* be required to notify the individual involved any time it discloses information about him to a third party from these databases. An identity thief can use the services of investigators and information brokers as easily as those with a legitimate need and lawful use for the information they provide. The following is the opt-out policy of US Search, as presented on its Web site (www.ussearch.com) in April 2003:

> US Search accesses numerous third party databases to gather information for our reports. We do not maintain the databases used in our searches; rather we access separately maintained third party databases to collect information for the reports we provide.
>
> If you would like to remove yourself from US Search reports you can do so by joining US Search's opt-out program. The opt-out program covers reports that contain non-public record information (sources like information compiled from magazine subscriptions) that is available for sale to the general public. US Search will use good faith efforts to help prevent your non-public record information from being distributed. We cannot provide any assurance that information that is otherwise public record information, such as court records, will be withheld. If you would like to be included in our opt-out program, you should contact us by mailing a signed request with the following information: your full name, e-mail address, mailing address, social security number, date of birth, past addresses and aliases to:
>
> **US Search.com Inc.**
> Opt-Out Program
> 5401 Beethoven Street
> Los Angeles, CA 90066

Unfortunately, other such companies do not provide any means for you to opt out of their selling of your nonpublic information. They simply gather information from whatever records they may be able to access, compile it in a database, and sell it to whoever wants to buy it. Because of these information brokers and thousands of smaller companies engaged in the same type of business, I recommend that anyone concerned about the crime of identity theft make a special effort to ensure that his or her personal information is contained in as few accessible databases as possible. Whenever an agency or business gives you the option of restricting access to information about you contained in its records or of opting out of the sharing of that information, I recommend that you take advantage of these opportunities to protect your personal privacy and safeguard yourself against the crime of identity theft.

# 4

# Take Control of How Your Private Financial Information Is Stored and Used

Early detection of identity theft is important to minimize the damage caused by the criminal who is using your personal and private information to commit his crimes. As mentioned previously, too often, the victim of identity theft is unaware that he has been victimized until several months or perhaps even a couple of years have passed.The identity thief is using your identity, opening accounts and accruing charges in your name, and you will probably remain completely unaware of his activities until you are denied credit or contacted by a bill collector demanding payment on these bad debts.

## CHECK YOUR CREDIT REPORTS

One of the best ways to keep track of what's going on with your credit is to review your credit reports on a regular basis. At a minimum, you should order a copy of your credit reports from the major credit reporting agencies once per year. Twice per year is better, and quarterly is the best option (although this can cost you up to $96 per year). It is important to obtain a report from each of the three major credit reporting agencies—Equifax, Experian, and TransUnion—because there may be information contained in one of these reports that is not in the others. Credit reports can be ordered conveniently online via the following Web sites:

**Equifax**
www.equifax.com

**TransUnion**
www.transunion.com

**Experian**
www.experian.com

Once you have a copy of your credit reports in hand, review each one carefully for accuracy and completeness. First and most importantly, make sure that every account listed on your credit report is one that you actually established. An account listed on your credit report that you do not recognize is a danger signal. It may be a simple error on the part of the credit reporting agency (and they make a bunch of them), or it may be that someone is using your name and personal identifying information to obtain credit and establish accounts in your name.

The next step is to make sure that any accounts listed as current/open are ones that you are actually using. That department store charge card that you applied for to get "15 percent off today's purchase" and that you used only once around Christmas two years ago may still be listed as an open account. You may have cut up the charge card and forgotten all about it, but the account is being carried as open by the department store and reported as such on your credit reports. An identity thief could take over this account and use it without your knowledge. If there are open accounts listed on your credit report that you are not using, close them. Simply call or send a letter to the business where you established the account and request that the account be closed.

Finally, look at the inquiries section of your credit report. Who has obtained information about you from your credit reports? Obviously if you have applied for credit, taken out a loan, or perhaps interviewed for a new job, there will be inquiries because your credit report is checked as a part of approving your credit or loan application or hiring you at your new job. However, *you should be very aware of any inquiries on your credit report that are not the result of an action you have taken.* If you are not in the market for a new car, you should not see credit inquiries from an automobile dealership. Likewise, if you're not purchasing a new Rolex watch or diamond ring, inquiries on your credit report from the Fly-by-Night Jewelry Company should serve as a warning.

Many companies that sell expensive products (e.g., automobile dealers) routinely run credit reports before making a sale. This makes perfect sense—they want to establish your creditworthiness before you drive away in a $40,000 vehicle. There is a problem only when your credit reports are being looked at by businesses with which you have no direct association. Remember, identity thieves have day jobs too . . . and may be working as used car sales reps.

You may find several inquiries on your credit report from companies with which you have no association because the major credit bureaus sell your personal financial information to companies that want to offer you credit. Although you may have never heard of these companies and have no interest in obtaining an additional credit card, your credit information was sold to them as part of a marketing scheme. Fortunately, however, there is a way to opt out of the selling of your private financial information and to limit the risk of identity theft associated with the disclosure of this information.

## OPT OUT OF CREDIT PRESCREENING: 1-888-5-OPT-OUT

When companies with which you have no association whatsoever buy your personal information from the major credit bureaus, they do so for the purpose of credit prescreening. Basically, how it works is that a company wanting to market its credit services to a group of people contacts a credit bureau to buy a list of prescreened potential customers. So Company X asks the credit bureau for a list of individuals living in, say, Los Angeles, all of whom make at least $50,000 per year, have at least one major credit card, and are married. The credit bureau consults its vast databases, puts together a list of people who meet these criteria and sells this list to Company X. Company X gives this list to its marketing department, which sends an offer for preapproved credit to all the names on the list.

If you have received an offer for a preapproved credit card, refinanced mortgage, or anything else along these lines in the mail, it is likely that preapproval was obtained by screening the private financial information contained in your credit reports.

If you don't want Company X obtaining information from your credit reports without your knowledge or permission, there is something you can do about it. You can opt out of this prescreening. That way, when Company X requests a list of people meeting certain conditions, your information won't be sold for use in its marketing scheme, even if you meet all of the conditions it is looking for. All you need to do to opt out is call the special toll-free number set up by the credit bureaus for this purpose: 1-888-5-OPT-OUT (1-888-567-8688). This is an automated service. You leave your identifying information, and the credit bureaus remove you from their prescreening lists.

As a step toward preventing identity theft, I strongly recommend that you take advantage of this free service. Besides the fact that the credit bureaus probably shouldn't be selling your personal information to companies with which you have no direct association, stopping these preapproved credit offers takes a tool away from the identity thief. Too often we view these offers as junk mail (which they are) and simply throw them away. But these offers are gold to an identity thief. An identity thief who gets his hands on one can complete the application with your information and his address and then sit back and await the arrival of his new credit card—in your name. Many of these offers for new credit cards come with three or four checks attached to the application so that you will have immediate access to your newly established line of credit. A criminal who finds this preapproved credit offer and associated checks, which you have tossed out as junk mail, can simply begin a bit of forgery in your name.

There is no disadvantage to opting out of this prescreening. If you decide you want to apply for credit with Company X, you can always submit an application. If you were approved in the prescreening, you will be approved when you submit an application yourself. The difference is, when you submit an application to Company X, you are making the conscious choice to disclose your personal information.

## ADD A FRAUD ALERT TO YOUR CREDIT REPORT

A fraud alert is a notice placed in your credit reports to alert credit grantors that you may be the victim of identity theft or fraud. Its purpose is to cause any credit grantor to obtain additional information to verify that requests for credit have actually come from you. This is normally accomplished by including your home telephone number in the fraud alert with the instruction that the credit grantor must obtain authorization from you by calling the telephone number provided before establishing any new account.

You do not need to wait until you have actually been victimized and suffered a major loss before placing a fraud alert on your credit reports. If you believe there is the potential of becoming the victim of an identity thief (remember, identity theft is one of the fastest growing crimes in America today) you should take this precaution. You simply need to contact the major credit bureaus listed below and instruct each one to place a fraud alert on your file.

**Equifax**
Consumer Fraud Division
P.O. Box 740256
Atlanta, GA 30374
www.equifax.com

**TransUnion**
Fraud Victim Assistance Department
P.O. Box 6790
Fullerton, CA 92834
www.transunion.com

**Experian**
National Consumer Assistance
P.O. Box 9530
Allen, TX 75013
www.experian.com

Prior to granting credit, most credit grantors will conduct a credit check on the applicant; however, they will not necessarily request a report from all three credit bureaus. It is thus important to have the fraud alert placed on each of your credit reports so that any potential credit grantor will see it. This is a simple procedure that takes about five minutes (after you actually get connected to a real person) with each credit bureau and is a significant step in protecting yourself from identity theft. The representative you speak with will ask you to answer some verifying questions (to prove you are who you say you are) and will then place the fraud alert on your credit file.

Is there any potential downside to having a fraud alert on your credit reports? Well, first it is important to understand that there is no law that requires a credit grantor to pay attention to a fraud alert. Fraud alerts can be and have been ignored by credit grantors. However, in the vast majority of cases a credit grantor will pay careful attention to a fraud alert. After all, it is in the credit grantor's interest to ensure that credit is being granted to the right person.

It is also important to understand that a fraud alert on your credit reports will limit your ability to gain "instant credit." Filling out that application for instant credit at the Acme Computer and Electronics Store, waiting while they do an online credit check, and then walking out with that new computer and no payments until 2014 just won't happen. Remember, a fraud alert stipulates that any creditor is supposed to contact you at the telephone number you have provided in the alert before granting credit. On the other hand, the fraud alert will prevent an identity thief from applying for that same instant credit in your name, walking out with that new computer, and leaving you to explain what happened when it comes time to make those payments.

## CALIFORNIA RESIDENTS: FREEZE YOUR BUREAU REPORT

A new California law, SB-168 (see Chapter 9), goes a long way toward allowing California residents to protect the content of their consumer credit files (credit reports) from disclosure. SB-168 does several things to protect California residents from identity theft, but one of the best things it does is enable them to place a "security freeze" on their credit reports. The security freeze is much more than a fraud alert. A fraud alert still allows your credit report (containing the alert notice) to be released. The security freeze prevents disclosure of your credit report itself. This means that your credit report is locked. It is frozen, and no information contained in it will be disclosed to anyone unless you specifically instruct the credit bureau to release it. (To allow access to your credit file, you will need to provide the credit bureau with proper identification, identify a password established by the credit bureau when the security freeze was placed, and specifically identify the third party to whom your credit information is to be released.)

Consumers should have a direct say regarding when and to whom their personal financial information is disclosed, and they should be able to prevent any disclosure of that information should they choose to do so. SB-168 allows California residents to take back control of their credit reports.

Each of the credit bureaus has slightly different procedures for placing a security freeze on the credit report of a California resident, and each charges a fee to do so. At the time this portion of SB-168 went into effect, the fee ranged from $12 to $59.95 (Equifax — $12, TransUnion — $29.95, Experian — $59.95). In short, however, it's simply a matter of contacting each of the credit bureaus, providing them with your California address, instructing them to apply a security freeze to your account, and, of course, paying the associated fee.

The benefits of placing a security freeze on your credit reports are obvious. No identity thief will be able to establish any type of major account in your name because no credit check can be performed in order to set up the account. Furthermore, it gives you absolute control over who gains access to your credit reports. But is there any downside to taking this precaution?

Placing a security freeze on your credit reports will result in the same basic problem as putting a fraud alert on your credit reports: you will limit your access to "instant credit" based on a quick online credit check. Beyond this, however, there is no real downside. Should you wish to allow access to your credit reports, the law provides that the credit bureaus must grant access to whomever you have instructed them to within three days. So if you plan to buy a new automobile, obtain a mortgage to purchase a home, or refinance a current account, the company needing access to your credit information can gain said access quickly once you give your permission. However, an identity thief, even knowing significant personal information about you, will not be able to gain access to your credit reports or allow others to do so in order to establish fraudulent accounts.

In addition, SB-168 provides some general protections for California residents. Specifically, it prohibits publicly posting or displaying Social Security numbers, printing Social Security numbers on identification cards, printing Social Security numbers on documents sent through the mail unless required by law or in applications for employment or credit, and requiring a person to transmit his or her Social Security number via an unencrypted Internet connection. In short, SB-168 tries to restrict the massive and uncontrolled use of Social Security numbers and protect California residents from the threat associated therewith.

In this author's opinion, SB-168 (while perhaps not all-encompassing) is definitely a step in the right direction in the effort to protect California residents against identity theft and associated crimes. If you are not a resident of California, you should encourage your own state legislature to adopt a similar law.

## INVOKE THE FINANCIAL SERVICES MODERNIZATION ACT (GRAMM-LEACH-BLILEY ACT)

In addition to the credit bureaus selling your personal financial information, your financial institutions (banks, credit unions, investment firms) are doing the same thing. As part of their marketing schemes, they are selling information about their customers to their affiliates as well as to completely unaffiliated companies.

If you believe that your financial institutions have a duty to protect your privacy, to safeguard your financial interest within the terms of your account, and to take no actions that would put you at risk of identity theft, fraud, or other financial crimes, I certainly agree with you. Unfortunately, your bank does not. Financial institutions have found that they can make money by selling your private information, and they do just that. The problem became so bad that the federal government finally stepped in.

Because of the risks posed to consumers by the blatant disclosure of their private financial information, Congress passed the Financial Services Modernization Act, or the Gramm-Leach-Bliley Act. It required all financial institutions to notify their customers of their rights under this law prior to July 2001. Most of them did this with a flyer included with your monthly bill along with the ads for current mortgage rates and new car loans. In this way, you were informed of your right to tell your financial institution that you did not want it to sell your private financial information (i.e., that you could opt out). If you did not exercise this right, however, financial institutions were free to continue selling it.

Thankfully, the law allows you to opt out *at any time*. To do so, you simply need to instruct your financial institutions to stop selling and sharing your personal financial information as required under the law.

It is very important to understand that the Financial Services Modernization Act is *not* specifically a privacy law. It is a financial services law that contains a privacy provision within its text. The act actually removed some of the barriers to the sharing of your private personal and financial information among banks, insurance companies, and the like. You can use the provisions of the law to limit disclosure of your private information, but you must take specific steps to do so. It is essential that you contact all of your financial service institutions and inform them that you do not want them selling or sharing your private information with others. Simply send the following letter to each of them:

Date

Your Name
Your Address

Financial Institution Name (Bank, Credit Card, Credit Union, Investment Broker, etc.)
Financial Institution Address

RE: Account Number(s) ______________________________

Dear Sir or Madam:

I am submitting the following instructions with regard to my account(s) and your information sharing and sales policies:

In accordance with the provisions of the Financial Services Modernization Act (Gramm-Leach-Bliley Act) allowing me to opt out of any sharing or selling of my personal information, I direct you NOT to share any of my personal identifiable information with non-affiliated third-party companies or individuals. I further direct you NOT to share nonpublic personal information about me with affiliated companies or individuals.

In accordance with the Fair Credit Reporting Act, allowing me to opt out of sharing of information about my creditworthiness, I direct you NOT to share information about my creditworthiness with any affiliate of your company.

I do NOT wish to receive marketing offers from you or your affiliates. Please immediately remove my name from all marketing lists and databases.

Thank you for your assistance in this matter and for taking steps to protect the privacy of your customers.

I request that you acknowledge receipt of these instructions and your intention to comply with my request for privacy of my personal, financial and other information by return mail.

Sincerely,
Your Signature
Your Name

# 5

# Safeguard Your Accounts

The identity thief wants to gain access to your accounts—your bank account, your credit card account, your utility accounts, and anything else that may give him access to information about you and allow him to make a profit from fraudulent use of that information.

Just as you protect your home from being burglarized by installing locks, lights, and alarms, you need to protect your accounts by establishing security procedures to prevent them from accessed by identity thieves.

Let's take a look at the various types of accounts you may have and what you can do to protect them.

## CREDIT CARDS

Credit cards provide a convenient way to make retail purchases, shop online, and carry a source of emergency funds. When used properly, a credit card is an asset that lets you maintain positive control over your purchases while at the same time offering protection against loss, theft, and fraud. The key phrase in the proceeding sentence is when used properly. Too often people use their credit cards improperly and neglect to take reasonable steps to protect their credit card accounts from compromise. As a result, they open themselves up to becoming the victims of an identity thief.

Let's take a bit more in-depth look at what you can do to protect yourself and your credit card accounts from identity theft.

### Keep a List of All Credit Card Accounts and Contact Information

If your credit cards were lost or stolen, how quickly could you report their loss? Do you have a copy of your credit card numbers along with their contact telephone numbers and addresses recorded and stored in a safe place? Contact information is recorded on the back of your credit cards and on your monthly statements, but if your credit cards have been stolen and you don't have a copy of your last statement handy, would you know whom to call? The more quickly you report a loss or theft of your credit cards, the more quickly these cards can be canceled to prevent their use by an identity thief.

I recommend that you make a simple list of your credit cards along with their account numbers and contact information to mitigate the damage that you would incur in the event that your wallet or purse was stolen and you lost your credit cards. Such a list will enable you to quickly report any lost or stolen credit cards and help prevent fraudulent charges from being made to your accounts. Store the list in a safe place in your home where you will have convenient access to it should you need to report the loss or theft of your credit cards.

#### Safeguard Your Accounts

| Acct. Name | Acct. Number | Telephone | Address |
|---|---|---|---|
| XYZ Visa | 0119 0112 2301 2519 | 1-800-555-1212 | 123 Main St.<br>Los Angeles, CA<br>90036 |
| ABC MasterCard | 0615 1810 1514 0913 | 1-800-555-0001 | 567 High St.<br>Atlanta, GA<br>39901 |
| ACME Dept. Store | 2512 1522 05 | 1- 800-555-1110 | 789 Acme Blvd.<br>Austin, TX 73301 |

It is important to record the "lost card" telephone number and *customer service address* on your list of credit card accounts. Often payments are sent to a payment-processing center, while all other matters regarding your account are handled by a customer service office at a different address. Sending a report of a lost or stolen credit card to the payment processing center will simply delay its arrival at the office that needs to process the information. *Remember, even after telephoning and reporting a lost or stolen credit card, you must follow up in writing.*

If you discover that your credit card has been lost or stolen, call the credit card issuer and report it immediately. Have them cancel your lost or stolen credit card and reissue you a new card with a new credit card number. Follow up with a letter to the credit card issuer, noting the date, the time, and the name of the person you spoke with when you reported this matter by telephone.

The major credit card companies all have national customer service telephone numbers that you can call for assistance with your credit cards and accounts. They may be able to assist you if your credit cards are lost or stolen and you have not recorded your account numbers and specific contact addresses for each card, but it will certainly be much easier if you take a moment to record your credit card information while you still have your cards in your possession.

## Do Not Carry Multiple Credit Cards on a Daily Basis

After obtaining one major credit card, many people obtain two or three others, along with various department store charge cards. Often these cards are all placed in this person's wallet or purse and carried around on a daily basis. This is not to say that the cards are used on a daily basis, only that they are carried. The problem comes about when this person's wallet or purse is lost or stolen. When this happens, all the credit cards must be canceled and reissued. Furthermore, there is a great likelihood that fraudulent charges will be made against all these cards before they can be canceled.

There is nothing wrong with having more than one credit card, but there is seldom any need to carry them all at the same time. Carry a single credit card with a very low limit for daily use. Leave your other, higher-limit credit cards locked up at home, and take them with you only when you know that you will be using them. I personally have a credit card with a $1,000 limit that I carry on a daily basis. This allows me to pay for small purchases, cover minor emergency automobile repairs, and the like, but if the card is lost or stolen it would very quickly reach its limit and thereafter be denied if an identity thief tried to use it. I also have a credit card with a much higher limit, which I use when I'm traveling and need to pay for airline tickets, rental cars, hotel rooms, and various things that would very quickly exceed the $1,000 limit of my daily-use credit card. The point here is that I don't risk losing multiple high-limit credit cards by carrying them all on a daily basis, and neither should you.

## Report Lost or Stolen Cards Immediately

OK, but what happens if your credit cards are lost or stolen? The very first thing you must do is contact your credit card company as soon as you discover that the cards are missing or that there are fraudulent charges being made to your account.

Obviously, if you are mugged and someone steals your wallet, you are immediately aware that your credit cards are now missing. Likewise, if you are shopping and try to pay with your credit card only to find that it is no longer in your possession, you are aware of its recent loss. However, it is important to remember that a criminal can make charges to your credit card without having actual possession of the card, as long as the criminal has certain information such as the credit card number, expiration date, and billing address. It is thus very important to review each charge on your credit card statement every month (not just the total owed or minimum payment owed) to ensure that there are no unauthorized charges.

No matter how you discover the theft, loss, or unauthorized use of your credit cards, you must all and report this to your credit card company without delay. Immediate reporting is essential not only to stop the unauthorized use of your credit cards but also to protect yourself from being held liable for the unauthorized charges.

Federal law provides that you may be held liable for no more than $50 per card if you report the unauthorized use immediately upon discovery. Furthermore, the major credit card companies have their own "zero-liability" policies, whereby they further protect their customers who have unauthorized charges made to their credit cards by waiving this first $50 fee.

Again, once you have made the call, it is essential that you follow up in writing. The following letter serves as a template for disputing fraudulent charges in writing. There is no specific requirement to use this exact format; you just need to be sure that you say when you reported the fraudulent charges by telephone and with whom you spoke. State your dispute clearly, ask that it be corrected immediately, and request that you be issued a new and corrected credit card statement.

The credit card company will begin an investigation of the fraudulent charges when you call, but it will need a written statement from you to correct the problem. You should mail your follow-up letter on the same day that you report the fraudulent charges by telephone. Be sure to keep a copy for your records.

---

Date: 1 February 2010

Your Name
Address
City, State, ZIP Code

Credit Card Company
Address
City, State, ZIP Code

Re: Account Number 5000 1234 5678 9000 –
DISPUTE OF FRAUDULENT CHARGES

Dear Sir or Madam:

This letter is a follow-up to my telephone conversation with your company on (DATE). During this telephone conversation I spoke with (NAME) and explained that unauthorized charges have been made to my credit card.

[Choose one of the following statements that best describes your dispute, or clearly state the problem in your own words.]

- Neither I, nor any person authorized by me to use my credit card, made the following charges: (DATE, AMOUNT, TYPE OF CHARGE). In addition, neither I, nor anyone authorized by me, received the goods or services represented by this transaction.
- I engaged in one transaction with this merchant on or about DATE in the amount of $$$. I have since been billed for transactions that I did not authorize. My card is still in my possession and has not been reported lost or stolen, nor was anyone else authorized to use my credit card.*

- I placed an order with the merchant on DATE; however, I have not received the merchandise or services paid for in this transaction. Expected delivery date was DATE. The merchant's response to my inquiries was_____________.*

*You must contact the merchant BEFORE disputing this charge with your credit card company.

Please remove this charge from my account immediately and credit my account with the amount of the unauthorized charge and any interest based on this charge.

I request that you provide me with a corrected account statement once you have corrected this error.

Sincerely,

Your Signature
Your Name

---

## Sign Your Credit Cards and Refuse Requests for Supplemental ID

Many people are writing the words "Check ID," "See ID," or something similar in place of their signature on the backs of their credit cards. They mistakenly believe that this somehow protects their credit cards against unauthorized use should they be lost or stolen.

The major credit card companies (Visa, MasterCard, American Express, etc.) are billion-dollar companies, each with extensive fraud-prevention departments. If requiring supplementary ID significantly reduced credit card fraud and identity theft, the credit card companies would certainly make supplementary ID a condition of using a credit card. The fact is, however, that "Check ID" or "See ID" written in place of an authorizing signature actually makes misuse of a lost or stolen credit card easier. Quoting from the Visa Fraud Awareness Training script:

"Unfortunately, there are some cardholders who think an unsigned card, or one with 'Check ID' written in the signature panel, is more secure. This is not true—it just allows criminals to sign the card or use a fake ID with their signature." Following is the full text of that script:

## Visa Merchant Fraud Awareness Training Script

Remember, a Visa card is not valid unless it is signed by the cardholder.

- Unfortunately, there are some cardholders who think an unsigned card, or one with "Check ID" written in the signature panel, is more secure. This is not true—it just allows criminals to sign the card, or use a fake ID with their signature.
- What if the signature panel instructs the merchant to "CHECK ID"?
- A card where the customer has written "CHECK ID" in the signature panel is considered an unsigned card.

**NOTE:**

- Effective January 1, 1998, the words "Not Valid Unless Signed" are printed near the signature panel on all Visa cards. This requirement provides merchants with an independent source to refer to when requesting that cardholders sign their cards, as well as justification for refusing to accept an unsigned card.

Most identity theft is NOT the result of some high-tech hacking into a secure database to steal your personal identifying information. According to the FTC's Bureau of Consumer Protection, the majority of identity theft occurs offline. Criminals committing identity theft gather your personal information from such things as carelessly discarded credit card receipts and mail delivered to an unlocked mailbox, or they get you to reveal your personal information directly.

The major credit card companies understand that requiring supplementary information as a condition of using your credit card puts you at risk. Furthermore, they understand that "Check ID" or "See ID" in place of your authorizing signature not only puts you at risk, but also puts the merchant accepting the card at risk. Any credit card without an authorizing signature is considered to be "unsigned" and is therefore invalid. No merchant should accept a credit card with the words "Check ID" or "See ID" in place of your signature.

I contacted Visa and asked for an explanation of the company's policies regarding requests for supplementary information as a condition of using a Visa card and the use of "See ID" in place of a signature. Visa's response to my inquiry follows:

> Thank you for your inquiry concerning a request for supplementary information for a Visa transaction. Merchants may not refuse to honor a Visa card simply because the cardholder refuses a request for supplementary information. The only exception is when a Visa card is unsigned when presented. However, "See ID" is not considered a valid signature. In these situations, a merchant must obtain authorization, review additional identification, and require the cardholder to sign the card before completing a transaction.
>
> Many cardholders have expressed concern about the recording of supplementary personal information on a bankcard sales draft. In response, several states have passed legislation that prohibits requiring such information on the transaction form. To find out if your state has passed such legislation, please contact your state legislator's office.
>
> Please notify the disputes area at the financial institution that services your account of any merchant practices that you feel are inappropriate. Your bank has access to the appropriate Visa rules and regulations as well as to the Notification of Customer Complaint forms which should be used by your bank to document and file merchant complaints. It is not necessary for your bank to be the offending merchant's financial institution in order to file a complaint for you.

You may also wish to contact the Visa Assistance Center at 1 800 VISA-911 to file your merchant complaint.

We hope this information proves helpful, and we thank you for using Visa.

Thank you for writing.

Visa Webmaster

---

There is absolutely no benefit whatsoever to not signing your credit cards, but there is certainly a risk to leaving them unsigned or using "Check ID" or "See ID" in place of your authorizing signature. Again, federal law limits your liability for unauthorized use of your credit cards, and the major credit card companies each have a "zero-liability policy" so that you have no liability for unauthorized use of your credit cards if they are lost or stolen. However, for these protections to apply, you must not have contributed to the unauthorized use.

There is a concept in the law known as "contributory negligence." *Black's Law Dictionary* (6th edition) defines contributory negligence as "The act or omission amounting to want of ordinary care on the part of complaining party, which, concurring with defendant's negligence is proximate cause of injury." Simply put, this means that you can't do something that contributes to your injury. You have a duty under the law to take reasonable precautions to protect yourself from harm and to mitigate harm that may occur.

The credit card companies require that credit card holder (you) sign their credit cards immediately upon receipt, and certainly prior to use. Failing to sign your credit card, or placing something in the signature block other than your signature (e.g., "Check ID" or "See ID"), contributes to any injury you may suffer should your credit card be lost or stolen. Likewise, any merchant that accepts an unsigned credit card or a credit card with something other than an authorizing signature in the signature block contributes to any injury that may be the result of a lost or stolen credit card being used by an identity thief.

It may be reasonably argued under the law that if you fail to sign your credit cards, use words such as "Check ID" or "See ID" in place of your signature, or provide unnecessary supplementary information to a merchant while using your credit card during a transaction, you are contributing to any injury you may suffer should fraudulent charges be made against your account. Simply put, you should no longer have limited liability under the law (or zero liability under the credit card companies' policies) if you fail to take the reasonable precautions of properly signing your credit card and refusing to provide supplemental ID when using it.

Credit cards are very useful tools, and like any tool, they must be used responsibly and safely. This, of course, means paying your debts in a timely manner, but it also means taking reasonable precautions to prevent misuse of your credit cards. To protect yourself from identity theft, properly sign all of your credit cards. If you currently have "Check ID" or some other foolishness in place of your signature, have your credit card issuer send you a new card and sign it properly immediately upon receipt. When you use your properly signed credit card to make a purchase, never submit to demands for ID or other supplementary information as a condition of the sale. If a merchant makes such demands, report this misconduct immediately to your credit card issuer.

## BANK ACCOUNTS

Establishing a bank account in your name is one of the primary goals of an identity thief. Not only does this allow him to access funds in your name, but it also serves as a form of secondary identification as he proceeds to steal more and more of your life. Let's take a look at how this can happen and ways to prevent it.

If an identity thief can obtain enough information about you, he can easily establish a bank account in your name. As noted previously, it is not all that difficult to do; after all, he's putting money *into* the bank, and banks want the business.

An identity thief will gather your personal information. He will know your name, address, telephone number, Social Security number, driver's license number (does this sound like information printed on your personal checks?), and date and place of birth.

Using this information, the identity thief first needs to obtain false identification in your name. Again, this is not particularly difficult. To open an account, the bank will usually want to see photo ID (such as a driver's license) and some secondary piece of ID, which can be pretty much anything else with your name on it. The identity thief presents false ID, completes the account application using your information, and provides the bank teller with an opening deposit—all in your name.

The identity thief now has a bank account established in your name, and you know nothing whatsoever about its existence. You may be wondering how this can happen. Simply put, the bank has no particular reason to be suspicious that the person opening an account and depositing money is some kind of criminal. Even assuming that a bank takes extra precautions to verify the identity of everyone opening an account, the identity thief has provided valid information about you. A credit check will confirm that you exist and that you have other established accounts and credit. A check with the DMV will confirm that the license number provided is valid and that it matches the name given by the identity thief (your name!). A check with the check verification companies will reveal that there is no derogatory information in their databases about you. A bank cannot reasonably be expected to conduct an extensive background check on every new customer, and the minimal checks it does make will confirm the story the identity thief is telling. After all, you've enabled an identity thief to learn your personal identifying information, and now he is able to use that information to convince others that he is you.

The identity thief doesn't open a bank account in your name because he wants to help you save a few dollars toward your retirement. He is using your good name and credit to open accounts in order to steal even more money than would be possible by stealing your existing credit cards or checkbook. Once he has opened this fraudulent bank account, he can use it as the basis for establishing other accounts and credit in your name. He can also transfer money from your actual accounts to the account he has established in your name and can then quickly withdraw the money and disappear.

The fraudulent bank account is difficult to guard against if you are careless in the disclosure of your personal information. Consider the ease with which you have been able to open a legitimate bank account in your own name. There is really no more difficulty doing so in the name of someone else, assuming that you have the necessary personal information about that person. This is why it is essential that you safeguard your personal information in order to prevent an identity thief from banking in your name.

## Use Personal Checks Wisely

Most people have checking accounts associated with one or more of their bank accounts. Checks offer a convenient way to access available funds, but they need to be used carefully and with forethought to prevent them from exposing the user to a risk of identity theft.

If I asked you to print your name, address, and telephone number on a piece of paper and give this piece of paper to a perfect stranger, would you do it? What if I asked you to add the name of your bank, your account number at the bank, and maybe your driver's license or Social Security number to this piece of paper, and then place your signature on it and give it all to some stranger? Would you do it?

Common sense says that you simply don't go around providing this type of information to strangers. You could rightly claim that writing all this information on a piece of paper and giving it to some stranger would put you at risk of fraud, identity theft, and related crimes.

Now think about what you do every time you write a personal check. Your checks, of course, identify your bank and your account number at the bank. You very likely have your name, address, and telephone number printed on your checks, and some people even have their driver's license number and/or Social Security number printed on their checks!

The same information that you would never write on a piece of paper and hand to some stranger is printed on your personal checks, which you hand to some stranger every time you use a check to make a retail purchase. Every time you write a personal check and hand it to some retail clerk, you put yourself at risk of fraud, identity theft, and related crimes.

Those of you who use checks to make retail purchases and who have the above information printed on your checks are likely thinking that this information has to be included on your check. No merchant will accept a check that doesn't contain sufficient identifying information about its drawer.

This is generally true if you present a check to a merchant in person. In most cases the merchant does not know you personally. You are asking him to accept your personal check and by default your personal guarantee that you have sufficient funds on deposit so that the check will clear the bank and the merchant will receive his money. The merchant insists on collecting significant personal information about you and recording that information on your personal check (or having it printed on the check to begin with) in order to track you down and demand payment if your check bounces (is returned for insufficient funds).

The problem is that every time you hand a personal check to a merchant you are providing significant personal information to a stranger. In fact, in some cases, you are providing enough information to allow yourself to be victimized by an identity thief. Remember that an identity thief very likely has a "normal" job somewhere. That retail clerk to whom you just handed your personal check may just supplement his income by stealing your identity.

To protect yourself against the crime of identity theft, you must safeguard your personal and private identifying data from unnecessary disclosure. This includes not having extensive personal information printed on your personal checks. For many years I have maintained a checking account where the only personal identifying information I have printed on my checks is my name. I have never had a problem with my checks being refused because my address, telephone number, driver's license number, and so on were not printed on them.

The reason for this easy acceptance of my personal checks is that I never use a personal check for direct, in-person retail purchases. Personal checks should only be used to send payment through the mail (i.e., to pay bills or make a purchase via mail order). In these cases, there is no need for extensive personal information to be printed on your checks. Any place where you have an established account will already have whatever information it needs from you to maintain your account. When you return the invoice along with your payment, it is processed along with every other payment. If you place an order for some item through the mail and pay with a personal check, there is again no need to have personal information printed on your check. Your order will be processed based on the order form sent with your order, not the information on your check. Most businesses will delay all orders paid by personal check until the check clears the bank anyway. Having personal information printed on your check does nothing to speed up delivery of your order.

There are certainly many people who use their checks to make direct, in-person retail purchases, but doing so puts them at risk of becoming a victim of identity theft. It is important to remember that, according to the FTC's Bureau of Consumer Protection, most identity theft occurs offline, with criminals obtaining data by stealing mail or recording it off of personal checks and carelessly discarded credit card receipts.

If you want to use funds from your checking account to make purchases, use an ATM/debit card to do so. Most businesses that accept personal checks are also set up to accept credit and debit cards. The use of a debit card adds a degree of security to your transaction because a PIN is generally required to complete the transaction. As long as you have not provided your PIN to anyone and have not written it down where it can be found along with your debit card, a thief cannot use your card to access your account.

It is important to note, however, that the security provided by an ATM PIN only applies to ATM cards that *do not* have a credit card (i.e., Visa or MasterCard) logo. ATM cards with a credit card logo can be processed as a credit transaction, thus requiring a signature but bypassing the need for a PIN. In this case the money is still automatically deducted from your checking account; it is just processed through the credit card system.

## What if Your Personal Check Is Rejected?

When a merchant accepts your personal check, he is taking a risk. The merchant must trust that your check is good, that when he deposits your check it will clear the bank and he will be credited with the funds for your purchase. Unfortunately, there are a lot of careless people who do not maintain sufficient balances in their checking accounts to cover the checks they write, and there are even more dishonest people who write checks knowing that their checks are bad and will likely bounce.

Because of the possibility that any given check accepted by a merchant will be bad, many merchants use a check verification service to help prevent or mitigate their losses from bad checks. A check verification company maintains a database of people who have written bad checks or have had their checking accounts closed as a result of writing bad checks. Merchants subscribe to these check verification services and, for a few cents per check, can compare information on a check with the information contained in the check verification company's database.

The various check verification companies have basic criteria for recommending approval or disapproval of a check (although the final decision is left to the merchant). The check verification company will first determine whether there is a history of bad checks being written on that account and whether the account is still open. It may also look at the number of checks it has been asked to approve from a given account on any one day. Some companies may have a limit of, say, five check approvals off a single account in any 24-hour period. The sixth check would not be approved.

Unfortunately, the databases of the check verification companies (like the databases of the major credit reporting agencies) are not perfect. Errors in data entry and database management do occur. However, if you find that your checks are being disapproved by a check verification service and you are certain that you have never bounced a check, there is a good possibility that someone else is using your personal information to cash checks. You may be the victim of identity theft!

As with the credit reporting agencies, you have a right to obtain a copy of any information held about you by the check verification companies. It is generally just a matter of contacting a check verification company and requesting a copy of any information they are maintaining about you. If you have had a check refused based on information provided by a check verification company, that company will provide a copy of your record to you for free.

Following is a list of those companies:

**CheckRite**
7050 Union Park Center #200
Midville, UT 84047

**ChexSystems**
Attn: Consumer Relations
12005 Ford Road, Suite 600
Dallas, TX 75234
www.chexhelp.com

**CrossCheck, Inc.**
P.O. Box 6008
Petaluma, CA 94955
www.cross-check.com

**National Processing Co. (NPC)**
Consumer Assistance
P.O. Box 379
Riverdale, NJ 07457
www.npc.net

**TeleCheck Services, Inc.**
5251 Westheimer
Houston, TX 77056
www.telecheck.com

**SCAN Shared Check Authorization Network**
Electronic Transaction Corp.
19803 North Creek Pkwy.
Bothell, WA 98011

# 6

# Businesses and Identity Theft

We tend to focus on identity theft as a crime that affects people, a crime against individuals. While this is accurate, it is also a crime against businesses.

When an identity thief steals someone's identity and makes a purchase with a fraudulent credit card at your business, you may find that these fraudulent charges are charged back against your merchant account as the individual victim of the crime attempts to restore his or her credit and reputation. An identity thief who opens a fraudulent checking account or simply steals checks from his victim and makes purchases or cashes these checks in your place of business may leave you holding a worthless piece of paper when the check bounces.

In addition, if your business

maintains records about your customers or potential customers and those records are lost or stolen, it may be rightly argued that you have a liability under the law for any damage caused due to negligence in failing to safeguard your customers' private information. Furthermore, if your business gains a reputation of being careless with customer information, you may find your customers taking their business elsewhere.

As a business owner or manager, you may want to consider the following ways to protect your business and your customers:

- Collect from customers only that information that you *specifically* need to conduct your business.
- If you must collect private or sensitive information from your customers in order to properly conduct your business, have a specific plan to safeguard this information. Store private and sensitive information in encrypted databases. Segregate private customer information from general customer information and restrict the private information to only employees who actually need the information to do their job.
- Establish a written privacy and security policy and be sure that all your employees are aware of it and follow it to the letter.
- Allow customers to opt out of any marketing or information sharing you engage in, or, better yet, establish an opt-in policy where you disclose no information about a customer and make no marketing contact with a customer without his express permission.
- Involve your customers in your privacy practices. For example, encourage customers to establish a password to protect their account information maintained by your business.
- If your business deals in retail sales, do not take personal checks from unknown customers. Provide your regular customers who want to use personal checks

with a check-cashing card/store prescreening of the validity of their accounts.

## THEFT AND LOSS OF RECORDS

Many businesses that maintain information about you in their databases have little direct use for much of the information they collect. These businesses and agencies maintain information for the purpose of establishing "customer profiles" with the intent of providing improved service to you. However, why a university needs the driver's license numbers of its students, or why a national video rental chain needs your Social Security number is really baffling.

Beyond the potential of misuse of your personal information by those maintaining the databases that contain it, there is the very real threat that these databases may be stolen, thereby compromising the personal information of every person listed therein and putting all these individuals at risk of identity theft and other like crimes.

On 14 December 2002, the office of TriWest Healthcare Alliance was broken into, and computer equipment containing the healthcare records of approximately 500,000 military members and their families was stolen. The databases on the stolen computer equipment contained not only confidential medical information but also identifying information about patients, including name, address, date of birth, and Social Security numbers. So . . . just what do Social Security numbers have to do with medical histories? In short, nothing. They are only included because the federal government has turned the Social Security number into a national identification number.

During February 2003, Kansas University posted a notice on its Web site warning that it had recently experienced a break-in and theft of "computer files that included names, Social Security numbers, dates of birth, and other details of personal information." Just why did Kansas University need to maintain the Social

Security numbers of its students in these computer files? There is certainly no requirement in the Social Security Act that colleges and universities maintain the Social Security numbers of their students, nor would students receive any less quality education by not disclosing their Social Security numbers to the university. However, every student whose personal information was stolen from Kansas University now faces a greatly increased risk of identity theft.

On 14 February 2003, Seattle's KING 5 News reported that hundreds of thousands of Washington state residents had their personal and confidential information compromised by the state's employment security department. It seems that the state of Washington, in selling some of its older computer equipment, hadn't bothered to remove a disk containing this confidential information. Thankfully, the person who purchased the surplus computer from the state was an honest man and returned the disk to the state. What's unfortunate about this case, however, is that it took this individual extra effort to return this confidential information to the state of Washington. According to the news report, "He called the state auditor's office to turn the disc in but no one ever called him back."

However, lest we think that Washington's employment security department is particularly careless, it is important to understand that the compromise of information in computer databases occurs on a regular and frequent basis. A 16 January 2003 report in the New Scientist.Com News Service revealed that Massachusetts Institute of Technology graduate students Simson Garfinkel and Abhi Shelat analyzed 158 secondhand computer hard drives purchased over the Internet between November 2000 and August 2002. Their analysis revealed more than 6,000 credit card numbers, e-mail, and other personal information. One of the hard drives analyzed by Garfinkel and Shelat had previously been part of an ATM and contained the account numbers and transaction information of 2,868 different customers.

It is important to recognize that these massive compromises

of personal and confidential information were not the result of highly skilled technologists, computer hackers, and programmers breaking encryption algorithms and defeating the security protocols protecting the data. In fact, just the opposite is true. The information was not compromised because someone beat the security protecting the databases but because *no security was in place*. Criminals simply crept through an open window or past an unsecured door and made off with the computer containing the data. Or a bumbling bureaucrat didn't bother to remove a disk containing this information before selling the computer as surplus, nor did the agency take the simple precaution of numbering and logging the disks containing confidential information. Finally, researchers simply purchased secondhand computers and read confidential data that nobody bothered to securely erase before selling the computer.

Whether it's a government agency or a private business gathering your personal information, there is seldom adequate security in place to protect the data once it is compiled into a database. Security costs money and can at times be inconvenient. Moreover, while no business or agency wants to have its databases compromised, the bottom line is that it suffers little if any liability if someone uses that information to steal your identity or commit crimes against you. If a criminal steals your identity because some business lost control of your personal information, you can bet that business won't be rushing to your aid as you fight to regain your identity and clear your good name.

# 7

# Identity Theft Prevention Quiz

Having gained some understanding about the crime of identity theft and looked at several things you can do to prevent it or mitigate its effects, you can now look at your specific vulnerabilities. The Identity Theft Prevention Quiz lets you evaluate your personal vulnerability to the crime of identity theft. How likely is it that you will become a victim?

Read each of the following statements. If the statement applies to you, add the number of points at the end of each statement to your total. After reading and evaluating each statement, compare your total points with the evaluation at the end of the quiz.

The point value assigned to each statement is based on the potential that the action described could increase your likelihood of becoming a victim of identity theft and the amount of personal control you have over each of the described actions.

- I carry my Social Security card (or other document containing my Social Security number) in my wallet or purse. (10 points)
- I have my Social Security number or driver's license number printed on my personal checks or allow these numbers to be written on my checks when I use them. (25 points)
- I have "Check ID" or a similar notation printed in place of my signature on my credit cards, or my credit cards are unsigned. (15 points)
- I provide supplementary identification when making a purchase with my properly signed credit card. (25 points)
- I use my Social Security number as my student or employee ID number. (5 points)
- My Social Security number is printed on my driver's license, and I have not requested that this be changed. (10 points)
- My Social Security number is my account number for any account other than Social Security. (10 points)
- I have not ordered a copy of my credit reports from all three major credit reporting agencies within the past year. (10 points)
- I have not notified my financial service providers (banks, credit cards, investment brokers, and so on) that I object to their releasing my information to third parties (in accordance with the Financial Services Modernization Act). (10 points)
- I provide my Social Security number whenever asked without knowing specifically why it is being requested and how it will be used. (20 points) (If you provided your Social Security number to a government agency

without obtaining a written copy of the Privacy Act, add an additional 5 points.)

- My telephone number is listed in the local telephone book or is available from directory assistance. (5 points)
- I receive mail in an unlocked box at my home or office. (15 points)
- I send mail by depositing it in an unlocked box for pick-up by my postal carrier or mail clerk (i.e., I do not mail my correspondence by depositing it in a USPS drop box or at the post office. (15 points)
- I do not have a list of all my credit card numbers and telephone contact telephone numbers and addresses for the issuers of these cards in a secure, locked location at home. (20 points)
- I have received two or more preapproved credit offers during the past month. (5 points) (If you threw these preapproved offers away without shredding them, add 20 points.)
- I do NOT have a paper shredder in my home. (10 points)
- I have not opted out of preapproved credit offers by calling 1-888-5-OPT-OUT. (10 points)
- I am not registered with the DMA Mail and Telephone Preference Services. (10 points)
- I provided information to or made a purchase from a telemarketer within the past six months. (20 points)
- I have responded to spam within the past six months. (20 points) (If you sent money or provided a credit card number, add 50 points.)
- I provide my personal information over nonsecure connections while shopping online. (25 points)
- I have the PIN for my ATM/debit cards written on the card or on something else carried with the cards in my wallet or purse. (50 points)
- I generally carry all (or most) of my credit cards in my

wallet or purse, whether I plan on using them that day or not. (10 points)
- I use the same PIN or password on more than one account. (15 points)

0 - 25 Points: You are probably quite aware of the threat of identity theft and have taken positive steps to protect yourself from this crime. Keep up the good work, but don't let your guard down.

25 - 75 Points: You are at risk! Some of your actions make it easy for an identity thief to target you. It's important to take steps to protect yourself from identity theft and to reduce the likelihood that you will be its next victim.

75 - 100+ Points: You are at extreme risk! During the next year, more than 1 million people will become victims of identity theft, and you are likely to be one of them. You may, in fact, already be a victim. It is essential that you take immediate steps to protect yourself from the crime of identity theft!

# 8

# You've Been Victimized—What Now?

It's happened. You have become the victim of an identity thief. What do you do?

Well, first off, don't panic. You have a serious problem, but it is a problem that can and will be solved over time. If you have read this book and followed the suggestions herein, you have already mitigated the damage that has been done. However, if you had taken steps to prevent becoming a victim of identity theft in advance you might have avoided it entirely, so we will assume that you are reading this book because you have already become a victim of the crime of identity theft.

It is important to clearly and fully understand that if you have your identity stolen you are the victim of a crime. Just as if you were mugged on the street or had your home burglarized, identity theft is a crime, and you are the victim of that crime.

Unfortunately, you—the victim—must undertake much of the recovery effort yourself. Unlike the victim of a mugging on the street or a burglary in a home, you may initially be seen as the perpetrator of a crime rather than its victim. When an identity thief runs up bills in your name, the bill collectors will see you as the deadbeat who skipped out on his debts. When an identity thief opens a checking account in your name and then bounces numerous checks, the bank and businesses where the bad checks were passed will initially come after you for this crime.

Though you are a victim of a crime, you will (at least initially) be seen as the criminal. Furthermore, you will be adjudged to be guilty of various crimes (credit card fraud, passing bad checks, etc.) until you are able to prove yourself innocent. Because of this, you must keep very detailed and precise records of every step you take in recovering from identity theft. The first of these steps is to establish a log to track your activities.

## KEEP A LOG

You will perform much if not all of the work required to recover from the crime of identity theft. It is absolutely essential that you keep very precise and accurate records of your actions in cleaning up the damage the identity thief has caused.

First, you should create a log to help you keep track of your actions. Your log will list the date of each action, the names and contact information of any people with whom you spoke, details on any correspondence you send or receive, any cost or fees you incur, and other notes that you feel may be useful.

The following chart on the next two pages is just an example of what your log might look like:

| DATE | CONTACT | COMMENTS |
|---|---|---|
| 23 February 2004 | John Smith | Received telephone call from ABC Collections demanding payment for an account they claim I have with Acme Corp. I explained that I have never had an account with Acme Corp. and requested they provide written documentation showing an account in my name. |
| 23 February 2004 | Paul Jones | Requested copy of my credit report from Equifax. |
| 23 February 2004 | Sally Smyth | Requested copy of my credit report from Experian. |
| 23 February 2004 | Bob Black | Requested copy of my credit report from TransUnion. |
| 23 February 2004 | Automated | Placed Fraud Alert on each of my credit reports. |
| 2 March 2004 | Mail | Received copy of Acme Corp. invoices from ABC Collections. |
| 3 March 2004 | Mail | Sent letter to ABC Collections disputing Acme Corp. charge as fraudulent. Certified Mail # 7000 1529 0002 0068 0899. |

| DATE | CONTACT | COMMENTS |
|---|---|---|
| 5 March 2004 | Mail | Received copy of credit reports from Equifax, Experian, and TransUnion. |
| 5 March 2004 | I.M. Cooper | Reported fraudulent accounts to police. Spoke with Detective I.M. Cooper, State Police Fraud Division. Got copy of police report #123-IDT-M03. |
| 6 March 2004 | Mail | Sent ID Theft Affidavit [see Appendix 1] to Equifax, Experian, and TransUnion. |
| 6 March 2004 | Jane Doe | Called XYZ Company to question fraudulent account listed on my TransUnion credit report. Requested written records of this account from XYZ Company. (1-800-555-0001) |

As you can see from the above example, this type of a log lets you easily keep track of your actions, the date of said actions, and the name of any person with whom you spoke. You will of course keep copies of any documents you send and receive, but the log provides you with a quick reference to your activities.

I believe that a detailed log is important in resolving the problems an identity thief has caused in your life. Once you become the victim of identity theft, it may take you several months or even years to get everything resolved. Trying to remember with whom you spoke at the XYZ Collection Agency three months ago or if you sent an ID Theft Affidavit (see Appendix 1) to the ABC Company is much easier if you track all of your recovery efforts in this way.

Finally, sometimes identity thieves get caught. An identity thief is a criminal and should be prosecuted for his crimes. Once an identity thief is arrested and brought before a judge and jury, your log will show the court the damage you suffered at the hands of this criminal and may enable you to recover some of your loss by order of the court.

## CONTACT THE CREDIT BUREAUS

As soon as you discover that you have become the victim of identity theft, you must contact the credit bureaus, obtain a copy of your credit reports, and place a fraud alert in your records. (It's actually a good idea to put a fraud alert—or, if you live in California, an SB-168 security freeze—in your records to help *prevent* identity theft.)

You should be reviewing your credit reports on a regular basis anyway, but if you have just discovered that one fraudulent account has been created in your name, there are likely to be others. If you have not already placed a fraud alert (or a security freeze) on your credit reports, doing so may prevent additional fraudulent accounts from being opened in your name.

Although listed elsewhere in this book, the addresses of the three major credit bureaus are listed here again for your convenience:

**Equifax**
P.O. Box 740241
Atlanta, GA 30374-0241
www.equifax.com

**Experian**
P.O. Box 9530
Allen, TX 75013
www.experian.com

**TransUnion**
P.O. Box 6790
Fullerton, CA 92634-6790
www.transunion.com

Carefully review each credit report for errors and fraudulent accounts. Report these errors to the appropriate credit bureaus and ask that they remove the inaccurate information from your credit reports. Because identity theft is such a growing crime, each of the credit bureaus has specialists trained to assist victims.

All correspondence with the credit bureaus should be in writing, but you may find it useful to discuss the fraudulent accounts with the specialists in the security/fraud preventions departments of each of the credit bureaus. These specialists can advise you on what additional information they may need to investigate fraudulent accounts. They can also provide contact information for the businesses originally listing the accounts on your credit report. Contact telephone numbers are generally included in the initial response you receive from the credit bureaus following your report of identity theft; however, you may want to request a contact number in your initial correspondence if speaking with a person at the credit bureau is important to you.

Once you report the inaccurate/fraudulent information to the credit bureaus, they must investigate the entries in question and either validate or remove them. This is a requirement under the federal Fair Credit Reporting Act and applies whether you are the victim of identity theft or simply the victim of poor database management on the part of the credit bureaus.

The credit bureaus have 30 days to investigate your report of errors in your credit report and make the necessary corrections. If their investigation results in changes to your credit report, they are also required to provide you with a free copy of your corrected report.

Although you will find that the credit bureaus are responsive (by federal law they must be), it will take the full 30 days in many cases for each disputed item to be investigated and the errors corrected. Remember, the credit bureaus have to go back to the business that originally reported the inaccurate information and allow that business time to investigate your dispute and respond. Only after this process is complete can the credit bureau make the corrections to your credit report. With this in mind, while the credit bureau is investigating your dispute, you may also want to contact the business that made the report and ask that it remove the false information from your credit report immediately (the business reported the information and can thus have it removed by telling the credit bureau it is in error).

Unfortunately, correcting fraudulent entries in your credit report is a slow process. Eventually the fraudulent entries will be removed, but while under investigation they will remain on your credit report, thus affecting your ability to obtain credit, employment, and other benefits associated with maintaining good credit.

## FILE A POLICE REPORT

Although identity theft is a rapidly increasing crime, it may not be a crime with which your local police department is prepared to deal. Many police departments see identity theft as a "civil matter" to be dealt with by the courts. Other departments may understand that identity theft is a crime but question whether it is within their jurisdiction. If you live in Los Angeles and an identity thief has opened a checking account and is writing checks in your name in San Francisco, do you report this to the Los Angeles police, the San Francisco police, the California state police, the FBI? What if the identity thief is writing bad checks in your name in Boston? You may find yourself caught in a never-ending circle as you are sent from one jurisdiction to the next because the various police departments all assume the jurisdiction for this crime belongs to some other agency.

It's not that most police officers aren't sympathetic to your problems, and if you could point out the bad guy and show reasonable evidence that he had committed a crime, almost any police officer would make every effort to catch and arrest him. The problem is that the police officer to whom you are reporting the identity theft may not really understand all that is involved here and may (rightly?) be focused on crimes of violence, such as murder, mugging, rape, and robbery.

The primary purpose of filing a police report is to aid you as you work to clear up the problems resulting from this crime. Having a copy of a police report that shows someone else obtained a driver's license in your name may help keep you from being arrested for actions committed by the identity thief posing as you. If an identity thief has opened accounts and run up fraudulent charges in your name, many businesses will want to see a copy of a police report before closing these accounts and absolving you of responsibility for these charges.

It is very important that you get the police to take a report and obtain a copy of that report along with the report number and the name of the police officer who filed it. Most (although not all) states have some law dealing with identity theft. You should be able to get the police to file a report as a violation of the identity theft laws in your state. If your state does not have specific laws dealing with identity theft, you should at least get the police to file a miscellaneous incident report.

Do not expect your local police department to conduct a massive investigation, however. They won't be assigning a team of their best detectives to the case, and the police commissioner certainly won't be canceling his Christmas vacation to take charge of the investigation.

That said, I do not want to disparage the effort of the police in tracking down and arresting identity thieves. Some departments have excellent fraud investigators. A department may even have a team that focuses on identity theft if a number of these crimes have been committed in its jurisdiction. Identity thieves do get identified, they do get arrested, and they do get convicted. It is, however, important to understand that the police have more than one crime to deal with and more than one victim to aid. When you report that you are the victim of the crime of identity theft, you can expect the police to help you—just don't expect too much.

## DEAL EFFECTIVELY WITH BILL COLLECTORS

After an identity thief has established accounts in your name and then skipped town, leaving the accounts unpaid, there are going to be a number of businesses looking to collect on these debts. After sending the first past-due notice, the second friendly reminder, a stern follow-up, and various demands for payment, many businesses will write these accounts off as bad debts and turn them over to some bill collection agency.

By the time a bill collector has these accounts, several months have likely passed since the identity thief first established the account in your name. The bill collector will use various investigative techniques to track you down (after all, the accounts are in your name) and will demand that you pay these debts and pay them NOW. Of course, this telephone call or letter from a bill collector demanding payment is probably the first time you have heard anything about these debts.

In responding to the bill collector, you should send a written response requesting a copy of all documentation related to this account. Don't accept a letter stating, "You owe the Acme Company $5,000—now pay up." You want copies of any applications used to establish the account, transactions history, and all other information they have on file regarding this account. You will need to review this information in order to clearly state that the account is not yours, and you will need the information in order to file a police report regarding the fraudulent accounts.

Most of the debts in the hands of bill collectors are the result of deadbeats skipping out on accounts they actually established and failing to pay debts they actually owe. Bill collectors have heard every excuse and delay tactic from people trying to avoid paying them . . . so don't expect a lot of sympathy from the bill collector as you try to explain that you are a victim of identity theft. Simply state that the account is not yours and request detailed information regarding the account before you will discuss it further. Do not sign any forms sent to you by a bill collector, make any type of deposit, or send in any "good faith" payments. Remember . . . although the bill collector is demanding payment from you, *this is not your debt*. You are a victim of the crime of identity theft.

Unfortunately, some bill collectors will not want to send you detailed information related to the debts they claim you owe, and more still will not stop their demands for payment even after you have stated that the debts are not yours. The bill collector may see this as simply a delay tactic and may have it fixed in his mind that you are little more than a deadbeat from whom he must extract payment of bad debts. There is, however, a federal law, the Fair Debt Collection Practices Act (FDCPA), that governs the conduct of bill collectors, and you should be aware of that law and its content.

One portion of the FDCPA relates to the validation of debts. Because you will be disputing debts established in your name by the identity thief, it is important to be familiar with it and to let the bill collector know that you are familiar with it. Section 809 of the FDCPA, Title 15 U.S.C 1601 et seq., reads as follows:

## § 809. Validation of debts [15 U.S.C. 1692g]

(a) Within five days after the initial communication with a consumer in connection with the collection of any debt, a debt collector shall, unless the following information is contained in the initial communication or the consumer has paid the debt, send the consumer a written notice containing—

(1) the amount of the debt;

(2) the name of the creditor to whom the debt is owed;

(3) a statement that unless the consumer, within thirty days after receipt of the notice, disputes the validity of the debt, or any portion thereof, the debt will be assumed to be valid by the debt collector;

(4) a statement that if the consumer notifies the debt collector in writing within the 30-day period that the debt, or any portion thereof, is disputed, the debt collector will obtain verification of the debt or a copy of a judgment against the consumer and a copy of such verification or judgment will be mailed to the consumer by the debt collector; and

(5) a statement that, upon the consumer's written request within the thirty-day period, the debt collector will provide the consumer with the name and address of the original creditor, if different from the current creditor.

(b) If the consumer notifies the debt collector in writing within the thirty-day period described in subsection (a) that the debt, or any portion thereof, is disputed, or that the consumer requests the name and address of the original creditor, the debt collector shall cease collection of the debt, or any disputed portion thereof, until the debt collector obtains verification of the debt or any copy of a judgment, or the name and address of the original creditor, and a copy of such verification or judgment, or name and address of the original creditor, is mailed to the consumer by the debt collector.

(c) The failure of a consumer to dispute the validity of a debt under this section may not be construed by any court as an admission of liability by the consumer.

A complete copy of the FDCPA is contained in Appendix 2 of this book.

Once you have the requested information from the bill collector, you should file a police report regarding the theft of your identity and the misuse of your accounts. Send a letter to the bill collector (you may want to use the Identity Theft Affidavit in Appendix 1) stating that the debt he is trying to collect from you is not your debt, and include a copy of the police report. In addition, you should inform the original creditor, in writing, that the debt is fraudulent. Ask the original creditor to provide you with any details available regarding the account in question.

In most cases, once you have informed the bill collector that the debt is not yours and provided supporting documentation in the form of the Identity Theft Affidavit and police report, this will be the last you hear from him or her regarding that particular debt. Bill collectors are, after all, trying to collect debts from people who legitimately owe said debts. It serves no purpose for a bill collector to pursue collection from a person who does not legitimately owe the debt.

In the rare case where a bill collector does continue to contact you, you can demand the cessation of all communication with you in accordance with the provisions of the FDCPA, which states:

> CEASING COMMUNICATION. If a consumer notifies a debt collector in writing that the consumer refuses to pay a debt or that the consumer wishes the debt collector to cease further communication with the consumer, the debt collector shall not communicate further with the consumer with respect to such debt. . . .

This should prevent further communication from the bill collector regarding this debt. If the bill collector does not cease communication with you after being instructed to do so, he is acting in violation of the law.

## HOW TO CLEAN UP THE MESS AND RESTORE YOUR GOOD NAME

If you have become the victim of an identity thief, clearing up the mess and restoring your good name will take considerable effort, but it's also important to remember that it can be done and that you will get your life back in time.

Among the greatest problems victims of identity theft face are discouragement and depression. It can seem as if the whole world has turned against you, when you know that you have done nothing wrong. Being hounded by bill collectors, being unable to obtain credit, and perhaps even losing your job or being arrested by police all because of the actions of an identity thief using your name can be very difficult to deal with alone. You should not hesitate to talk with close friends and family about the problems you are facing and your feelings about it. If necessary, don't forget that professional counseling is available for victims of crime and may be something of which you want to avail yourself.

It is also important to remember that it will take time to restore your good name after being victimized by an identity thief. This will be little comfort when you are listening to a loan officer deny your application for a loan or sitting in a jail cell as the police try to sort out your identity from that of an identity thief, but remember, it *will* get resolved.

It is not uncommon for victims of identity theft to suffer some fairly significant emotional problems. Every telephone call may be a bill collector demanding payment of some new bill. Every day when the mail carrier delivers your mail, you may find further demands for payment of debts that are not yours or other correspondence that must be dealt with as a result of the actions of an identity thief.

The invasion of privacy and disruption of life caused by an identity thief can (and often does) leave the victim in a state of constant stress and worry regarding his financial security, the safety of his family, and his inability to conduct the simple transactions that are part of normal daily life. In many cases, the victim of identity theft is left with a feeling of utter helplessness because he has no idea what steps to take to recover from the crime and mitigate its effects.

Fortunately, having read this book, you will know what steps to take to begin restoring your good name, which will help to alleviate some of that feeling of helplessness. However, it is important to understand that being the victim of a crime puts you on an emotional roller coaster that won't end just because you have been absolved of responsibility for the fraudulent accounts established by the identity thief in your name.

As you are working to recover from the effects of this crime, it is essential that you take time to discuss your feelings with your family and listen to their feelings as well. Remember, the stress and emotional disruption you are feeling is normal, but it is important that you don't let it destroy your family life.

Remember, you are the victim of a crime, but you *will* recover from it.

# 9

# Know the Law

There are various laws, both state and federal, that specifically relate to identity theft. Although this book is not a law book, nor is it intended to provide legal advice, it is often helpful to be able to read the text of specific laws and know where to locate other laws related to your situation. This will help you understand the specifics of the crimes committed against you as well as your rights and protections under the law. Furthermore, when dealing with the police, government agencies, and various businesses, you may find that they may not really have any understanding of the laws related to identity theft. It is often helpful to be able to cite specific laws and requirements under those laws when working to recover your good name.

Whether you are recovering from identity theft or taking steps to prevent becoming a victim of identity theft, it is important to understand what the law actually says regarding this crime.

We will begin by looking at federal law.

## FEDERAL LAW ADDRESSING IDENTITY THEFT

### IDENTITY THEFT AND ASSUMPTION DETERRENCE ACT

As amended by Public Law 105-318, 112 Stat. 3007 (Oct. 30, 1998)

---

An Act

To amend chapter 47 of title 18, United States Code, relating to identity fraud, and for other purposes. [NOTE: Oct. 30, 1998 - [H.R. 4151]

Be it enacted by the Senate and House of Representatives of the United States of America in Congress assembled, [NOTE: Identity Theft and Assumption Deterrence Act of 1998.]

Sec.
001. Short Title
002. Constitutional Authority to Enact this Legislation
003. Identity Theft
004. Amendment of Federal Sentencing Guidelines for Offenses Under Section 1028
005. Centralized Complaint and Consumer Education Service for Victims of Identity Theft
006. Technical Amendments to Title 18, United States Code
007. Redaction of Ethics Reports Filed by Judicial Officers and Employees

§ 001. Short Title. [NOTE: 18 U.S.C. 1001 note.]

This Act may be cited as the "Identity Theft and Assumption Deterrence Act of 1998".

§ 002. Constitutional Authority to Enact this Legislation. [NOTE: 18 U.S.C. 1028 note.]

The constitutional authority upon which this Act rests is the power of Congress to regulate commerce with foreign nations and among the several States, and the authority to make all laws which shall be necessary and proper for carrying into execution the powers vested by the Constitution in the Government of the United States or in any department or officer thereof, as set forth in article I, section 8 of the United States Constitution.

§ 003. Identity Theft.

(a) Establishment of Offense.—Section 1028(a) of title 18, United States Code, is amended—

(1) in paragraph (5), by striking "or" at the end;
(2) in paragraph (6), by adding "or" at the end;
(3) in the flush matter following paragraph (6), by striking "or attempts to do so,"; and
(4) by inserting after paragraph (6) the following:

"(7) knowingly transfers or uses, without lawful authority, a means of identification of another person with the intent to commit, or to aid or abet, any unlawful activity that constitutes a violation of Federal law, or that constitutes a felony under any applicable State or local law;".

(b) Penalties.—Section 1028(b) of title 18, United States Code, is amended—

(1) in paragraph (1)—

(A) in subparagraph (B), by striking "or" at the end;
(B) in subparagraph (C), by adding "or" at the end; and
(C) by adding at the end the following:

"(D) an offense under paragraph (7) of such subsection that involves the transfer or use of 1 or more means of identification if, as a result of the offense, any individual committing the offense obtains anything of value aggregating $1,000 or more during any 1-year period;";

(2) in paragraph (2)—

(A) in subparagraph (A), by striking "or transfer of an identification document or" and inserting ", transfer, or use of a means of identification, an identification document, or a"; and
(B) in subparagraph (B), by inserting "or (7)" after "(3)";

(3) by amending paragraph (3) to read as follows:

"(3) a fine under this title or imprisonment for not more than 20 years, or both, if the offense is committed—
"(A) to facilitate a drug trafficking crime (as defined in section 929(a)(2));
"(B) in connection with a crime of violence (as defined in section 924(c)(3)); or
"(C) after a prior conviction under this section becomes final;";

(4) in paragraph (4), by striking "and" at the end;
(5) by redesignating paragraph (5) as paragraph (6); and
(6) by inserting after paragraph (4) the following:

"(5) in the case of any offense under subsection (a), forfeiture to the United States of any personal property used or intended to be used to commit the offense; and".

(c) Circumstances.—Section 1028(c) of title 18, United States Code, is amended by striking paragraph (3) and inserting the following:

"(3) either—

"(A) the production, transfer, possession, or use prohibited by this section is in or affects interstate or foreign commerce; or
"(B) the means of identification, identification document, false identification document, or document-making implement is transported in the mail in the course of the production, transfer, possession, or use prohibited by this section.".

(d) Definitions.—Subsection (d) of section 1028 of title 18, United States Code, is amended to read as follows:

"(d) In this section—

"(1) the term 'document-making implement' means any implement, impression, electronic device, or computer hardware or software, that is specifically configured or primarily used for making an identification document, a false identification document, or another document-making implement;
"(2) the term 'identification document' means a document made or issued by or under the authority of the United States Government, a State, political subdivision of a State, a foreign government, political subdivision of a foreign government, an international governmental or an international quasi-governmental organization which, when completed with information concerning a particular individual, is of a type intended or commonly accepted for the purpose of identification of individuals;
"(3) the term 'means of identification' means any name or number that may be used, alone or in conjunction with any other information, to identify a specific individual, including any—

"(A) name, social security number, date of birth, official State or

government issued driver's license or identification number, alien registration number, government passport number, employer or taxpayer identification number;
"(B) unique biometric data, such as fingerprint, voice print, retina or iris image, or other unique physical representation;
"(C) unique electronic identification number, address, or routing code; or
"(D) telecommunication identifying information or access device (as defined in section 1029(e));

"(4) the term 'personal identification card' means an identification document issued by a State or local government solely for the purpose of identification;
"(5) the term 'produce' includes alter, authenticate, or assemble; and
"(6) the term 'State' includes any State of the United States, the District of Columbia, the Commonwealth of Puerto Rico, and any other commonwealth, possession, or territory of the United States.".

(e) Attempt and Conspiracy.—Section 1028 of title 18, United States Code, is amended by adding at the end the following:

"(f) Attempt and Conspiracy.—Any person who attempts or conspires to commit any offense under this section shall be subject to the same penalties as those prescribed for the offense, the commission of which was the object of the attempt or conspiracy.".

(f) Forfeiture Procedures.—Section 1028 of title 18, United States Code, is amended by adding at the end the following:

"(g) Forfeiture Procedures.—The forfeiture of property under this section, including any seizure and disposition of the property and any related judicial or administrative proceeding, shall be governed by the provisions of section 413 (other than subsection (d) of that section) of the Comprehensive Drug Abuse Prevention and Control Act of 1970 (21 U.S.C. 853).".

(g) Rule of Construction.—Section 1028 of title 18, United States Code, is amended by adding at the end the following: "(h) Rule of Construction.—For purpose of subsection (a)(7), a single identification document or false identification document that contains 1 or more means of identification shall be construed to be 1 means of identification.".

(h) Conforming Amendments.—Chapter 47 of title 18, United States Code, is amended—

(1) in the heading for section 1028, by adding "and information" at the end; and
(2) in the table of sections at the beginning of the chapter, in the item relating to section 1028, by adding "and information" at the end.

§ 004. Amendment of Federal Sentencing Guidelines for Offenses Under Section 1028. [NOTE: 28 U.S.C. 994 note.]

(a) In General.—Pursuant to its authority under section 994(p) of title 28, United States Code, the United States Sentencing Commission shall review and amend the Federal sentencing guidelines and the policy statements of the Commission, as appropriate, to provide an appropriate penalty for each offense under section 1028 of title 18, United States Code, as amended by this Act.
(b) Factors for Consideration.—In carrying out subsection (a), the United States Sentencing Commission shall consider, with respect to each offense described in subsection (a)—

(1) the extent to which the number of victims (as defined in

section 3663A(a) of title 18, United States Code) involved in the offense, including harm to reputation, inconvenience, and other difficulties resulting from the offense, is an adequate measure for establishing penalties under the Federal sentencing guidelines;
(2) the number of means of identification, identification documents, or false identification documents (as those terms are defined in section 1028(d) of title 18, United States Code, as amended by this Act) involved in the offense, is an adequate measure for establishing penalties under the Federal sentencing guidelines;
(3) the extent to which the value of the loss to any individual caused by the offense is an adequate measure for establishing penalties under the Federal sentencing guidelines;
(4) the range of conduct covered by the offense;
(5) the extent to which sentencing enhancements within the Federal sentencing guidelines and the court's authority to sentence above the applicable guideline range are adequate to ensure punishment at or near the maximum penalty for the most egregious conduct covered by the offense;
(6) the extent to which Federal sentencing guidelines sentences for the offense have been constrained by statutory maximum penalties;
(7) the extent to which Federal sentencing guidelines for the offense adequately achieve the purposes of sentencing set forth in section 3553(a)(2) of title 18, United States Code; and
(8) any other factor that the United States Sentencing Commission considers to be appropriate.

§ 005. Centralized Complaint and Consumer Education Service for Victims of Identity Theft. [NOTE: 18 USC 1028 note.]

(a) In <<NOTE: Deadline.>> General.—Not later than 1 year after the date of enactment of this Act, the Federal Trade Commission shall establish procedures to—

(1) log and acknowledge the receipt of complaints by individuals who certify that they have a reasonable belief that 1 or more of their means of identification (as defined in section 1028 of title 18, United States Code, as amended by this Act) have been assumed, stolen, or otherwise unlawfully acquired in violation of section 1028 of title 18, United States Code, as amended by this Act;
(2) provide informational materials to individuals described in paragraph (1); and
(3) refer complaints described in paragraph (1) to appropriate entities, which may include referral to—

(A) the 3 major national consumer reporting agencies; and
(B) appropriate law enforcement agencies for potential law enforcement action.

(b) Authorization of Appropriations.—There are authorized to be appropriated such sums as may be necessary to carry out this section.

§ 006. Technical Amendments to Title 18, United States Code.

(a) Technical Correction Relating to Criminal Forfeiture Procedures.--Section 982(b)(1) of title 18, United States Code, is amended to read as follows: "(1) The forfeiture of property under this section, including any seizure and disposition of the property and any related judicial or administrative proceeding, shall be governed by the provisions of section 413 (other than subsection (d) of that section) of the Comprehensive Drug Abuse Prevention and Control Act of 1970 (21 U.S.C. 853).".
(b) Economic Espionage and Theft of Trade Secrets as Predicate Offenses for Wire Interception.—Section 2516(1)(a) of title 18, United States Code, is amended by inserting "chapter 90 (relating to protection of trade secrets)," after "to espionage),".

§ 007. Redaction of Ethics Reports Filed by Judicial Officers and Employees.

Section 105(b) of the Ethics in Government Act of 1978 (5 U.S.C.App.) is amended by adding at the end the following new paragraph:

"(3)(A) This section does not require the immediate and unconditional availability of reports filed by an individual described in section 109(8) or 109(10) of this Act if a finding is made by the Judicial Conference, in consultation with United States Marshall Service, that revealing personal and sensitive information could endanger that individual.
"(B) A report may be redacted pursuant to this paragraph only—

"(i) to the extent necessary to protect the individual who filed the report; and
"(ii) for as long as the danger to such individual exists.

"(C) The Administrative Office of the United States Courts shall submit to the Committees on the Judiciary of the House of Representatives and of the Senate an annual report with respect to the operation of this paragraph including—

"(i) the total number of reports redacted pursuant to this paragraph;
"(ii) the total number of individuals whose reports have been redacted pursuant to this paragraph; and
"(iii) the types of threats against individuals whose reports are redacted, if appropriate.

"(D) The Judicial Conference, in consultation with the Department of Justice, shall issue regulations setting forth the circumstances under which redaction is appropriate under this

paragraph and the procedures for redaction.[NOTE: Regulations.]
"(E) This paragraph shall expire on December 31, 2001, and apply to filings through calendar year 2001.". [NOTE: Expiration date.]

Approved October 30, 1998.

---

LEGISLATIVE HISTORY—H.R. 4151 (S. 512):

SENATE REPORTS: No. 105-274 accompanying S. 512 (Comm. on the Judiciary).

CONGRESSIONAL RECORD, Vol. 144 (1998):

Oct. 7, considered and passed House.
Oct. 14, considered and passed Senate.

WEEKLY COMPILATION OF PRESIDENTIAL DOCUMENTS, Vol. 34 (1998):

Oct. 30, Presidential statement.

## CALIFORNIA LAW ADDRESSING IDENTITY THEFT

Now let's review one of the better laws on the books with regard to preventing identity theft. This is a California state law and is thus only applicable in California; however, SB-168 is a good example of some current legislation that actually works to stop identity theft (and, of course, if you happen to live in California it is directly applicable to you).

## CALIFORNIA LAW SB-168, IDENTITY THEFT PREVENTION

SB-168 (Bowen) - The Identity Theft Prevention Act provides for security alerts and freezes on credit reports, effective July 1, 2002 through July 1, 2005. The purpose of SB-168 is to provide individuals with some degree of control over the information contained in their credit files and to provide specific restrictions on the display of Social Security numbers. The law itself is clearly written and easy to understand. It is quoted hereinafter for your reference.

## THE PEOPLE OF THE STATE OF CALIFORNIA DO ENACT AS FOLLOWS:

SECTION 1. Section 1785.11.1 is added to the Civil Code, to read:

1785.11.1. (a) A consumer may elect to place a security alert in his or her credit report by making a request in writing or by telephone to a consumer credit reporting agency. "Security alert" means a notice placed in a consumer's credit report, at the request of the consumer, that notifies a recipient of the credit report that the consumer's identity may have been used without the consumer's consent to fraudulently obtain goods or services in the consumer's name.
(b) A consumer credit reporting agency shall notify each person requesting consumer credit information with respect to a consumer of the existence of a security alert in the credit report of that consumer, regardless of whether a full credit report, credit score, or summary report is requested.
(c) Each consumer credit reporting agency shall maintain a toll-free telephone number to accept security alert requests from consumers 24 hours a day, seven days a week.
(d) The toll-free telephone number shall be included in any written disclosure by a consumer credit reporting agency to any consumer pursuant to Section 1785.15 and shall be printed

in a clear and conspicuous manner.
(e) A consumer credit reporting agency shall place a security alert on a consumer's credit report no later than five business days after receiving a request from the consumer.
(f) The security alert shall remain in place for at least 90 days, and a consumer shall have the right to request a renewal of the security alert.

SEC. 2. Section 1785.11.2 is added to the Civil Code, to read:
1785.11.2. (a) A consumer may elect to place a security freeze on his or her credit report by making a request in writing by certified mail to a consumer credit reporting agency. "Security freeze" means a notice placed in a consumer's credit report, at the request of the consumer and subject to certain exceptions, that prohibits the consumer credit reporting agency from releasing the consumer's credit report or any information from it without the express authorization of the consumer. When a security freeze is in place, information from a consumer's credit report shall not be released to a third party without prior express authorization from the consumer. This subdivision does not prevent a consumer credit reporting agency from advising a third party that a security freeze is in effect with respect to the consumer's credit report.
(b) A consumer credit reporting agency shall place a security freeze on a consumer's credit report no later than five business days after receiving a written request from the consumer.
(c) The consumer credit reporting agency shall send a written confirmation of the security freeze to the consumer within 10 business days and shall provide the consumer with a unique personal identification number or password to be used by the consumer when providing authorization for the release of his or her credit for a specific party or period of time.
(d) If the consumer wishes to allow his or her credit report to be accessed for a specific party or period of time while a freeze is in place, he or she shall contact the consumer credit

reporting agency, request that the freeze be temporarily lifted, and provide the following:
(1) Proper identification, as defined in subdivision (c) of Section 1785.15.
(2) The unique personal identification number or password provided by the credit reporting agency pursuant to subdivision (c).
(3) The proper information regarding the third party who is to receive the credit report or the time period for which the report shall be available to users of the credit report.
(e) A consumer credit reporting agency that receives a request from a consumer to temporarily lift a freeze on a credit report pursuant to subdivision (d), shall comply with the request no later than three business days after receiving the request.
(f) A consumer credit reporting agency may develop procedures involving the use of telephone, fax, the Internet, or other electronic media to receive and process a request from a consumer to temporarily lift a freeze on a credit report pursuant to subdivision (d) in an expedited manner.
(g) A consumer credit reporting agency shall remove or temporarily lift a freeze placed on a consumer's credit report only in the following cases:
(1) Upon consumer request, pursuant to subdivision (d) or (j).
(2) If the consumer's credit report was frozen due to a material misrepresentation of fact by the consumer. If a consumer credit reporting agency intends to remove a freeze upon a consumer's credit report pursuant to this paragraph, the consumer credit reporting agency shall notify the consumer in writing prior to removing the freeze on the consumer's credit report.
(h) If a third party requests access to a consumer credit report on which a security freeze is in effect, and this request is in connection with an application for credit or any other use, and the consumer does not allow his or her credit report to be accessed for that specific party or period of time, the third party may treat the application as incomplete.

(i) If a consumer requests a security freeze, the consumer credit reporting agency shall disclose the process of placing and temporarily lifting a freeze, and the process for allowing access to information from the consumer's credit report for a specific party or period of time while the freeze is in place.

(j) A security freeze shall remain in place until the consumer requests that the security freeze be removed. A consumer credit reporting agency shall remove a security freeze within three business days of receiving a request for removal from the consumer, who provides both of the following:

(1) Proper identification, as defined in subdivision (c) of Section 1785.15.

(2) The unique personal identification number or password provided by the credit reporting agency pursuant to subdivision (c).

(k) A consumer credit reporting agency shall require proper identification, as defined in subdivision (c) of Section 1785.15, of the person making a request to place or remove a security freeze.

(l) The provisions of this section do not apply to the use of a consumer report by the following:

(1) A person or entity, or a subsidiary, affiliate, or agent of that person or entity, or an assignee of a financial obligation owing by the consumer to that person or entity, or a prospective assignee of a financial obligation owing by the consumer to that person or entity in conjunction with the proposed purchase of the financial obligation, with which the consumer has or had prior to assignment an account or contract, including a demand deposit account, or to whom the consumer issued a negotiable instrument, for the purposes of reviewing the account or collecting the financial obligation owing for the account, contract, or negotiable instrument. For purposes of this paragraph, "reviewing the account" includes activities related to account maintenance, monitoring, credit line increases, and account upgrades and enhancements.

(2) A subsidiary, affiliate, agent, assignee, or prospective assignee of a person to whom access has been granted under subdivision (d) of Section 1785.11.2 for purposes of facilitating the extension of credit or other permissible use.
(3) Any state or local agency, law enforcement agency, trial court, or private collection agency acting pursuant to a court order, warrant, or subpoena.
(4) A child support agency acting pursuant to Chapter 2 of Division 17 of the Family Code or Title IV-D of the Social Security Act (42 U.S.C. et seq.).
(5) The State Department of Health Services or its agents or assigns acting to investigate Medi-Cal fraud.
(6) The Franchise Tax Board or its agents or assigns acting to investigate or collect delinquent taxes or unpaid court orders or to fulfill any of its other statutory responsibilities.
(7) The use of credit information for the purposes of prescreening as provided for by the federal Fair Credit Reporting Act.
(m) Nothing in this act shall prevent a consumer credit reporting agency from charging a reasonable fee to a consumer who elects to freeze, remove the freeze, or temporarily lift the freeze regarding access to a consumer credit report, except that a consumer reporting agency may not charge a fee to a victim of identity theft who has submitted a valid police report or valid Department of Motor Vehicles investigative report that alleges a violation of Section 530.5 of the Penal Code.

SEC. 3. Section 1785.11.3 is added to the Civil Code, to read:
1785.11.3. (a) If a security freeze is in place, a consumer credit reporting agency shall not change any of the following official information in a consumer credit report without sending a written confirmation of the change to the consumer within 30 days of the change being posted to the consumer's file: name, date of birth, social security number, and address. Written confirmation is not required for technical modifications of a consumer's official information, including name and street abbreviations, com-

plete spellings, or transposition of numbers or letters. In the case of an address change, the written confirmation shall be sent to both the new address and to the former address.
(b) If a consumer has placed a security alert, a consumer credit reporting agency shall provide the consumer, upon request, with a free copy of his or her credit report at the time the 90-day security alert period expires.

SEC. 4. Section 1785.11.4 is added to the Civil Code, to read:
1785.11.4. The provisions of Sections 1785.11.1, 1785.11.2, and 1785.11.3 do not apply to a consumer credit reporting agency that acts only as a reseller of credit information pursuant to Section 1785.22 by assembling and merging information contained in the database of another consumer credit reporting agency or multiple consumer credit reporting agencies, and does not maintain a permanent database of credit information from which new consumer credit reports are produced. However, a consumer credit reporting agency acting pursuant to Section 1785.22 shall honor any security freeze placed on a consumer credit report by another consumer credit reporting agency.

SEC. 5. Section 1785.11.6 is added to the Civil Code, to read:
1785.11.6. The following entities are not required to place in a credit report either a security alert, pursuant to Section 1785.11.1, or a security freeze, pursuant to Section 1785.11.2:
(a) A check services company, which issues authorizations for the purpose of approving or processing negotiable instruments, electronic funds transfers, or similar methods of payments.
(b) A demand deposit account information service company, which issues reports regarding account closures due to fraud, substantial overdrafts, ATM abuse, or similar negative information regarding a consumer, to inquiring banks or other financial institutions for use only in reviewing a consumer request for a demand deposit account at the inquiring bank or financial institution.
SEC. 6. Section 1785.15 of the Civil Code is amended to read:

1785.15. (a) A consumer credit reporting agency shall supply files and information required under Section 1785.10 during normal business hours and on reasonable notice. In addition to the disclosure provided by this chapter and any disclosures received by the consumer, the consumer has the right to request and receive all of the following:
(1) Either a decoded written version of the file or a written copy of the file, including all information in the file at the time of the request, with an explanation of any code used.
(2) A credit score for the consumer, the key factors, and the related information, as defined in and required by Section 1785.15.1.
(3) A record of all inquiries, by recipient, which result in the provision of information concerning the consumer in connection with a credit transaction that is not initiated by the consumer and which were received by the consumer credit reporting agency in the 12-month period immediately preceding the request for disclosure under this section.
(4) The recipients, including end users specified in Section 1785.22, of any consumer credit report on the consumer which the consumer credit reporting agency has furnished:
(A) For employment purposes within the two-year period preceding the request.
(B) For any other purpose within the 12-month period preceding the request. Identification for purposes of this paragraph shall include the name of the recipient or, if applicable, the fictitious business name under which the recipient does business disclosed in full. If requested by the consumer, the identification shall also include the address of the recipient.
(b) Files maintained on a consumer shall be disclosed promptly as follows:
(1) In person, at the location where the consumer credit reporting agency maintains the trained personnel required by subdivision (d), if he or she appears in person and furnishes proper identification.

(2) By mail, if the consumer makes a written request with proper identification for a copy of the file or a decoded written version of that file to be sent to the consumer at a specified address. A disclosure pursuant to this paragraph shall be deposited in the United States mail, postage prepaid, within five business days after the consumer's written request for the disclosure is received by the consumer credit reporting agency. Consumer credit reporting agencies complying with requests for mailings under this section shall not be liable for disclosures to third parties caused by mishandling of mail after the mailings leave the consumer reporting agencies.
(3) A summary of all information contained in files on a consumer and required to be provided by Section 1785.10 shall be provided by telephone, if the consumer has made a written request, with proper identification for telephone disclosure.
(4) Information in a consumer's file required to be provided in writing under this section may also be disclosed in another form if authorized by the consumer and if available from the consumer credit reporting agency. For this purpose a consumer may request disclosure in person pursuant to Section 1785.10, by telephone upon disclosure of proper identification by the consumer, by electronic means if available from the consumer credit reporting agency, or by any other reasonable means that is available from the consumer credit reporting agency.
(c) "Proper identification," as used in subdivision (b) means that information generally deemed sufficient to identify a person. Only if the consumer is unable to reasonably identify himself or herself with the information described above, may a consumer credit reporting agency require additional information concerning the consumer's employment and personal or family history in order to verify his or her identity.
(d) The consumer credit reporting agency shall provide trained personnel to explain to the consumer any information furnished him or her pursuant to Section 1785.10.
(e) The consumer shall be permitted to be accompanied by

one other person of his or her choosing, who shall furnish reasonable identification. A consumer credit reporting agency may require the consumer to furnish a written statement granting permission to the consumer credit reporting agency to discuss the consumer's file in that person's presence.

(f) Any written disclosure by a consumer credit reporting agency to any consumer pursuant to this section shall include a written summary of all rights the consumer has under this title and in the case of a consumer credit reporting agency which compiles and maintains consumer credit reports on a nationwide basis, a toll-free telephone number which the consumer can use to communicate with the consumer credit reporting agency. The written summary of rights required under this subdivision is sufficient if in substantially the following form: "You have a right to obtain a copy of your credit file from a consumer credit reporting agency. You may be charged a reasonable fee not exceeding eight dollars ($8). There is no fee, however, if you have been turned down for credit, employment, insurance, or a rental dwelling because of information in your credit report within the preceding 60 days. The consumer credit reporting agency must provide someone to help you interpret the information in your credit file.

You have a right to dispute inaccurate information by contacting the consumer credit reporting agency directly. However, neither you nor any credit repair company or credit service organization has the right to have accurate, current, and verifiable information removed from your credit report. Under the Federal Fair Credit Reporting Act, the consumer credit reporting agency must remove accurate, negative information from your report only if it is over seven years old. Bankruptcy information can be reported for 10 years. If you have notified a consumer credit reporting agency in writing that you dispute the accuracy of information in your file, the consumer credit reporting agency must then, within 30 business days, reinvestigate and modify or remove inaccurate information. The consumer credit reporting agency may not charge a fee for this service. Any pertinent information and copies of all documents you have concerning an error should be given to the consumer credit reporting agency.

If reinvestigation does not resolve the dispute to your satisfaction, you may send a brief statement to the consumer credit reporting agency to keep in your file, explaining why you think the record is inaccurate. The consumer credit reporting agency must include your statement about disputed information in a report it issues about you.

You have a right to receive a record of all inquiries relating to a credit transaction initiated in 12 months preceding your request. This record shall include the recipients of any consumer credit report.

You may request in writing that the information contained in your file not be provided to a third party for marketing purposes.

You have a right to place a "security alert" in your credit report, which will warn anyone who receives information in your credit report that your identity may have been used without your consent and that recipients of your credit report are advised, but not required, to verify your identity prior to issuing credit. The security alert may prevent credit, loans, and services from being approved in your name without your consent. However, you should be aware that taking advantage of this right may delay or interfere with the timely approval of any subsequent request or application you make regarding a new loan, credit, mortgage, insurance, rental housing, employment, investment, license, cellular phone, utilities, digital signature, Internet credit card transaction, or other services, including an extension of credit at point of sale. If you place a security alert on your credit report, you have a right to obtain a free copy of your credit report at the time the 90-day security alert period expires. A security alert may be requested by calling the following toll-free telephone number: (Insert applicable toll-free telephone number).

You have a right to place a "security freeze" on your credit report, which will prohibit a consumer credit reporting agency from releasing any information in your credit report without your express authorization. A security freeze must be requested in writing by certified mail. The security freeze is designed to prevent credit, loans, and services from being approved in your name without your consent. However, you should be aware that using a security freeze to take control over who gets access to the personal and financial information in your credit report may delay, interfere with, or prohibit the timely approval of any subsequent request or application you make regarding a new loan, credit, mortgage, insurance, government services or payments rental housing, employment, investment, license, cellular phone, utilities, digital signature, Internet credit card transaction, or other services, including an extension of credit at point of sale. When you place a security freeze on your credit report, you will be provided a personal identification number or password to use if you choose to remove the freeze on your credit report or authorize the release of your credit report for a specific party or period of time after the freeze is in place. To provide that authorization you must contact the consumer credit reporting agency and provide all of the following:

(1) The personal identification number or password.

(2) Proper identification to verify your identity.

(3) The proper information regarding the third party who is to receive the credit report or the period of time for which the report shall be available.

A consumer credit reporting agency must authorize the release of your credit report no later than three business days after receiving the above information.

A security freeze does not apply to a person or entity, or its affiliates, or collection agencies acting on behalf of the person or entity, with which you have an existing account, that requests information in your credit report for the purposes of reviewing or collecting the account. Reviewing the account includes activities related to account maintenance, monitoring, credit line increases, and account upgrades and enhancements. You have a right to bring civil action against anyone, including a consumer credit reporting agency, who improperly obtains access to a file, knowingly or willfully misuses file data, or fails to correct inaccurate file data."

SEC. 7. Title 1.81.1 (commencing with Section 1798.85) is added to Part 4 of Division 3 of the Civil Code, to read:

TITLE 1.81.1. CONFIDENTIALITY OF SOCIAL SECURITY NUMBERS

1798.85. (a) A person or entity, not including a state or local agency, shall not do any of the following:
(1) Publicly post or publicly display in any manner an individual's social security number. "Publicly post" or "publicly display" means to intentionally communicate or otherwise make available to the general public.
(2) Print an individual's social security number on any card required for the individual to access products or services provided by the person or entity.
(3) Require an individual to transmit his or her social security number over the Internet unless the connection is secure or the social security number is encrypted.
(4) Require an individual to use his or her social security number to access an Internet Web site, unless a password or unique personal identification number or other authentication device is also required to access the Web site.
(5) Print an individual's social security number on any materials that are mailed to the individual, unless state or federal law requires the social security number to be on the document to be mailed. Notwithstanding this provision, applications and forms sent by mail may include social security numbers.
(b) Except as provided in subdivision (c), subdivision (a) applies only to the use of social security numbers on or after July 1, 2002.

(c) Except as provided in subdivision (f), a person or entity, not including a state or local agency, that has used, prior to July 1, 2002, an individual's social security number in a manner inconsistent with subdivision (a), may continue using that individual's social security number in that manner on or after July 1, 2002, if all of the following conditions are met:

(1) The use of the social security number is continuous. If the use is stopped for any reason, subdivision (a) shall apply.

(2) The individual is provided an annual disclosure, commencing in the year 2002, that informs the individual that he or she has the right to stop the use of his or her social security number in a manner prohibited by subdivision (a).

(3) A written request by an individual to stop the use of his or her social security number in a manner prohibited by subdivision (a) shall be implemented within 30 days of the receipt of the request. There shall be no fee or charge for implementing the request.

(4) A person or entity, not including a state or local agency, shall not deny services to an individual because the individual makes a written request pursuant to this subdivision.

(d) This section does not prevent the collection, use, or release of a social security number as required by state or federal law or the use of a social security number for internal verification or administrative purposes.

(e) This section does not apply to documents that are recorded or required to be open to the public pursuant to Chapter 3.5 (commencing with Section 6250), Chapter 14 (commencing with Section 7150) or Chapter 14.5 (commencing with Section 7220) of Division 7 of Title 1 of, or Chapter 9 (commencing with Section 54950) of Part 1 of Division 2 of Title 5 of, the Government Code. This section does not apply to records that are required by statute, case law, or California Rule of Court, to be made available to the public by entities provided for in Article VI of the California Constitution.

(f) (1) In the case of a health care service plan, a provider of

health care, an insurer or a pharmacy benefits manager, or a contractor as defined in Section 56.05, this section shall become operative in the following manner:
(A) On or before January 1, 2003, the entities listed in paragraph (1) of subdivision (f) shall comply with paragraphs (1), (3), (4), and (5) of subdivision (a) as these requirements pertain to individual policyholders.
(B) On or before January 1, 2004, the entities listed in paragraph (1) of subdivision (f) shall comply with paragraphs (1) to (5), inclusive, of subdivision (a) as these requirements pertain to new individual policyholders and new employer groups issued on or after January 1, 2004.
(C) On or before July 1, 2004, the entities listed in paragraph (1) of subdivision (f) shall comply with paragraphs (1) to (5), inclusive, of subdivision (a) for all policyholders and for all enrollees of the Healthy Families and Medi-Cal programs, except that individual and employer group policyholders in existence prior to January 1, 2004, shall comply upon their renewal date, but no later than July 1, 2005.
(2) A health care service plan, a provider of health care, an insurer or a pharmacy benefits manager, or a contractor shall make reasonable efforts to cooperate, through systems testing and other means, to ensure that the requirements of this article are implemented on or before the dates specified in this section.
(3) Notwithstanding paragraph (2), the Director of the Department of Managed Health Care, pursuant to the authority granted under Section 1346 of the Health and Safety Code, or the Insurance Commissioner, pursuant to the authority granted under Section 12921 of the Insurance Code, and upon a determination of good cause, may grant extensions not to exceed six months for compliance by health care service plans and insurers with the requirements of this section when requested by the health care service plan or insurer. Any extension granted shall apply to the health care service plan or insurer's affected providers, pharmacy benefits manager, and contractors.

(g) If a federal law takes effect requiring the United States Department of Health and Human Services to establish a national unique patient health identifier program, a provider of health care, a health care service plan, a licensed health care professional, or a contractor, as those terms are defined in Section 56.05, that complies with the federal law shall be deemed in compliance with this section.

SEC. 8. Section 1 of this act shall become operative on July 1, 2002. Sections 2 and 3 of this act shall become operative on January 1, 2003.

Clearly, SB-168 provides some significant protections to individuals and helps to shield them from the crime of identity theft. Although only directly applicable to California residents, this law can serve as an example of legislation you may want to discuss with your elected representatives and propose as a law in your state of residence.

## OTHER STATE LAWS

The majority of states have some type of law specifically dealing with the crime of identity theft. Space prohibits reproducing copies of all those laws here; however, I recommend that you obtain a copy of the law pertaining to identity theft for the state in which you maintain your residence. Most libraries or your local city hall should be able to assist you in obtaining a copy of the appropriate legislation for your state.

Having a copy of your state's law pertaining to identity theft allows you to gain a better understanding of how this crime is viewed in your state. If you should ever become a victim of identity theft, it is helpful to be able to cite this law when dealing with the police and other government agencies.

The citation for each state's law is listed on the following pages:

| | |
|---|---|
| Alabama | Alabama Code § 13A-8-190 through 201 |
| Alaska | Alaska Stat § 11.46.565 |
| Arizona | Ariz. Rev. Stat. § 13-2008 |
| Arkansas | Ark. Code Ann. § 5-37-227 |
| California | Cal. Penal Code § 530.5-8 |
| Colorado | Does not have a specific ID theft law. |
| Connecticut | Conn. Stat. § 53a-129a (criminal)<br>Conn. Stat. § 52-571h (civil) |
| Delaware | Del. Code Ann. tit. II, § 854 |
| Florida | Fla. Stat. Ann. § 817.568 |
| Georgia | Ga. Code Ann. § 16-9-120, through 128 |
| Hawaii | HI Rev. Stat. § 708-839.6-8 |
| Idaho | Idaho Code § 18-3126 (criminal)<br>Idaho Code § 28-51-102 (civil) |
| Illinois | 720 Ill. Comp. Stat. 5/16 G |
| Indiana | Ind. Code § 35-43-5-3.5 |
| Iowa | Iowa Code § 715A.8 (criminal)<br>Iowa Code § 714.16.B (civil) |
| Kansas | Kan. Stat. Ann. § 21-4018 |
| Kentucky | Ky. Rev. Stat. Ann. § 514.160 |
| Louisiana | La. Rev. Stat. Ann. § 14:67.16 |
| Maine | ME Rev. Stat. Ann. tit. 17-A § 905-A |
| Maryland | Md. Code Ann. art. 27 § 231 |
| Massachusetts | Mass. Gen. Laws ch. 266, § 37E |

| | |
|---|---|
| Michigan | Mich. Comp. Laws § 750.285 |
| Minnesota | Minn. Stat. Ann. § 609.527 |
| Mississippi | Miss. Code Ann. § 97-19-85 |
| Missouri | Mo. Rev. Stat. § 570.223 |
| Montana | Mon. Code Ann. § 45-6-332 |
| Nebraska | NE Rev. Stat. § 28-608 & 620 |
| Nevada | Nev. Rev. State. § 205.463-465 |
| New Hampshire | N.H. Rev. Stat. Ann. § 638:26 |
| New Jersey | N.J. Stat. Ann. § 2C:21-17 |
| New Mexico | N.M. Stat. Ann. § 30-16-24.1 |
| New York | NY CLS Penal § 190.77-190.84 |
| North Carolina | N.C. Gen. Stat. § 14-113.20-23 |
| North Dakota | N.D.C.C. § 12.1-23-11 |
| Ohio | Ohio Rev. Code Ann. § 2913.49 |
| Oklahoma | Okla. Stat. Title 21, § 1533.1 |
| Oregon | Or. Rev. Stat. § 165.800 |
| Pennsylvania | 18 Pa. Cons. State § 4120 |
| Rhode Island | R.I. Gen. Laws § 11-49.1-1 |
| South Carolina | S.C. Code Ann. § 16-13-500, 501 |
| South Dakota | S.D. Codified Laws § 22-30A-3.1. |
| Tennessee | TCA § 39-14-150 (criminal)<br>TCA § 47-18-2101 (civil) |
| Texas | Tex. Penal Code § 32.51 |
| Utah | Utah Code Ann. § 76-6-1101-1104 |

| | |
|---|---|
| Vermont | Does not have a specific ID Theft law. |
| Virginia | Va. Code Ann. § 18.2-186.3 |
| Washington | Wash. Rev. Code § 9.35.020 |
| West Virginia | W. Va. Code § 61-3-54 |
| Wisconsin | Wis. Stat. § 943.201 |
| Wyoming | Wyo. Stat. Ann. § 6-3-901 |

APPENDIX

# 1

# Identity Theft Affidavit

The FTC developed the Identity Theft Affidavit in conjunction with retailers, consumer organizations, and privacy rights groups to simplify the process of disputing debts and fraudulent accounts opened by an identity thief.

Many companies officially endorse the Identity Theft Affidavit as the basis for reporting fraudulent accounts opened in one's name. Even those companies who have not specifically endorsed the Identity Theft Affidavit are very likely to accept it, since it provides all the necessary information a company would require to begin an investigation of such accounts and make a decision on a claim.

As of 19 December 2002, the following companies had officially endorsed the Identity Theft Affidavit and were listed on the FTC Web site as having done so:

5Star Bank
Aardvarkpr.com
ACA International
Altoona Postal Employees Credit Union
Amcrin Corporation
American Bankers Association
American Contracting Exchange
America's Community Bankers
Arkansas Federal Credit Union
AT&T
Atlantic Credit Union
Bank of Alameda
Bank of America
BankersOnline.com
Bankers Trust Company, N.A.
Call for Action
Capital One
Chase Manhattan Bank
Coastal Federal Credit Union
Computer Sciences Corporation
Corporate America Family Credit Union
Council of Better Business Bureaus
Credit Bureau of East Tennessee, Inc.
Digital e Group, Inc.
Direct Marketing Association
E-Privex.Com Inc.
Equifax
Experian
Federal Reserve Board
Fifth Third Bank
First National Bank Omaha
Fleet Boston Financial
Florida Telco Credit Union
GE Capital
GetThere LP
Gold Quest Realty, LTD. CO.
Identity Theft Resource Center

Intersections, Inc.
Investors Savings Bank
Iowa Independent Bankers
Key Federal Credit Union
Kimberly Clark Credit Union
Kleberg First National Bank
Marine Credit Union
Merrill Lynch
Michigan State University ID Theft Partnership for Prevention
Mountain View Federal Credit Union
National Association of Federal Credit Unions
New York Institute of Legal Research
Nexity Bank
Nextreme Services
Nissan Motor Acceptance Corporation
Oregon Telco Community Credit Union
Privacy Guard
Privacy Rights Clearinghouse
Provident Credit Union
Providian
SBC Service
SCE Federal Credit Union
Sears
Sun Country Credit Union
Terrace Security Company
The California Office of Privacy Protection
The Simpson Organization, Inc.
Thurman & Thurman Publications
TransUnion
Tri-County Debt Management of CWO, Inc.
U.S. Bank
U.S. Postal Inspection Service
Virginia Office of the Attorney General
VW Credit
Western Capital
Western Funding.com
Yolo Community Bank

## INSTRUCTIONS FOR COMPLETING THE ID THEFT AFFIDAVIT

To make certain that you do not become responsible for the debts incurred by the identity thief, you must provide proof that you didn't create the debt to each of the companies where accounts were opened or used in your name.

This ID Theft Affidavit was developed to help you report information to many companies using just one standard form. Use of this affidavit is optional for companies. While many companies accept this affidavit, others require that you submit more or different forms. Before you send the affidavit, contact each company to find out if they accept it.

You can use this affidavit where a *new account* was opened in your name. The information will enable the companies to investigate the fraud and decide the outcome of your claim. (If someone made unauthorized charges to an *existing account*, call the company to find out what to do.)

This affidavit has two parts:

1. **ID Theft Affidavit**, where you report general information about yourself and the theft.
2. **Fraudulent Account Statement**, where you describe the fraudulent account(s) opened in your name. Use a separate Fraudulent Account Statement for each company you need to write to.

When you send the affidavit to the companies, attach *copies* (not originals) of any supporting documents (e.g., driver's license, police report) you have. Before submitting your affidavit, review the disputed account(s) with family members or friends who may have information about the account(s) or access to them.

Complete this affidavit as soon as possible. Many creditors ask that you send it within two weeks of receiving it. Delaying could slow the investigation.

*Be as accurate and complete as possible.* You *may* choose not to provide some of the information requested. However, incorrect or incomplete information will slow the process of investigating your claim and absolving the debt. Please print clearly.

When you have finished completing the affidavit, mail a copy to each creditor, bank, or company that provided the thief with the unauthorized credit, goods, or services you describe. Attach to each affidavit a copy of the fraudulent account statement with information only on accounts opened at the institution receiving the packet, as well as any other supporting documentation you are able to provide.

*Send the appropriate documents to each company by certified mail, return receipt requested,* so you can prove that they were received. The companies will review your claim and send you a written response informing you of the outcome of their investigation. *Keep a copy of everything you submit for your records.*

If you cannot complete the affidavit, a legal guardian or someone with power of attorney may complete it for you. Except as noted, the information you provide will be used only by the company to process your affidavit, investigate the events you report, and help stop further fraud. If this affidavit is requested in a lawsuit, the company might have to provide it to the requesting party.

Completing this affidavit does not guarantee that the identity thief will be prosecuted or that the debt will be cleared.

If you haven't already done so, report the fraud to the following organizations:

- Each of the three national consumer reporting agencies. Ask each agency to place a fraud alert on your credit report and send you a copy of your credit file. When you have completed your affidavit packet, you may want to send them a copy to help them investigate the disputed accounts.

**Equifax**
P.O. Box 740241
Atlanta, GA 30374-0241
www.equifax.com

**Experian**
P.O. Box 9530
Allen, TX 75013
www.experian.com

**TransUnion**
Fraud Victim Assistance Division
P.O. Box 6790
Fullerton, CA 92634-6790
www.transunion.com

- The fraud department at each creditor, bank, or utility/service that provided the identity thief with unauthorized credit, goods, or services. This would be a good time to find out if the company accepts this affidavit and whether it requires notarization or a copy of the police report.
- Your local police department. Ask the officer to take a report and give you a copy of the report. Sending a copy of your police report to financial institutions can speed up the process of absolving you of wrongful debts or removing inaccurate information from your credit reports. If you can't get a copy, at least get the number of the report.
- The FTC, which maintains the Identity Theft Data Clearinghouse—the federal government's centralized identity theft complaint database—and provides information to identity theft victims at www.consumer.gov/idtheft. The FTC collects complaints from identity theft victims and shares their information with law enforcement nationwide. This information also may be shared with other government agencies, consumer reporting agencies, and companies where the fraud was perpetrated to help resolve identity-theft-related problems.

# ID THEFT AFFIDAVIT

## Victim Information

(1) My full legal name is

______________________________________________

(First) (Middle) (Last) (Jr., Sr., III)

(2) (If different from above) When the events described in this affidavit took place, I was known as

______________________________________________

(First) (Middle) (Last) (Jr., Sr., III)

(3) My date of birth is ____________________
(day/month/year)

(4) My Social Security number is

______________________________________________

(5) My driver's license or identification card state and number are

______________________________________________

(6) My current address is

______________________________________________

City ______________________ State ______ Zip ____________

(7) I have lived at this address since ______________________
(month/year)

(8) (If different from above) When the events described in this affidavit took place, my address was

______________________________________________

City ______________________ State ______ Zip ____________

(9) I lived at the address in Item 8 from__________until__________
(month/year) (month/year)

(10) My daytime telephone number (____)__________________
My evening telephone number (____)__________________

## How the Fraud Occurred

**Check all that apply for items 11–17:**

(11) _____ I did not authorize anyone to use my name or personal information to seek the money, credit, loans, goods or services described in this report.

(12) _____ I did not receive any benefit, money, goods or services as a result of the events described in this report.

(13) _____ My identification documents (for example, credit cards; birth certificate; driver's license; Social Security card; etc.) were ___ stolen ___ lost on or about __________________.
(day/month/year)

(14) _____ To the best of my knowledge and belief, the following person(s) used my information (for example, my name, address, date of birth, existing account numbers, Social Security number, mother's maiden name, etc.) or identification documents to get money, credit, loans, goods, or services without my knowledge or authorization:

| | |
|---|---|
| Name (if known) | Name (if known) |
| Address (if known) | Address (if known) |
| Phone number(s) (if known) | Phone number(s) (if known) |

________________________________________________

________________________________________________

________________________________________________

________________________________________________

________________________________________________

________________________________________________

| Additional information (if known) | Additional information (if known) |
|---|---|

(15) _____ I do NOT know who used my information or identification documents to get money, credit, loans, goods, or services without my knowledge or authorization.

(16) _____ Additional comments: (For example, description of the fraud, which documents or information were used, or how the identity thief gained access to your information.)

________________________________________________

________________________________________________

________________________________________________

________________________________________________

________________________________________________

________________________________________________

________________________________________________

________________________________________________

(Attach additional pages as necessary.)

## Victim's Law Enforcement Actions

(17) (check one) I _____ am _____ am not willing to assist in the prosecution of the person(s) who committed this fraud.

(18) (check one) I _____ am _____ am not authorizing the release of this information to law enforcement for the purpose of assisting them in the investigation and prosecution of the person(s) who committed this fraud.

(19) (check all that apply) I _____ have _____ have not reported the events described in this affidavit to the police or other law enforcement agency. The police _____ did_____ did not write a report.

*In the event you have contacted the police or other law enforcement agency, please complete the following:*

______________________________________________

**(Agency #1)** (Officer/Agency personnel taking report)

______________________________________________

(Date of report) (Report number, if any)

______________________________________________

(Phone number) (E-mail address, if any)

______________________________________________

**(Agency #2)** (Officer/Agency personnel taking report)

______________________________________________

(Date of report) (Report number, if any)

______________________________________________

(Phone number) (E-mail address, if any)

## Documentation Checklist

Please indicate the supporting documentation you are able to provide to the companies you plan to notify. Attach copies (not originals) to the affidavit before sending it to the companies.

(20) _____ A copy of a valid government-issued photo identification card (for example, your driver's license, state-issued ID card, or passport). If you are under 16 and don't have a photo ID, you may submit a copy of your birth certificate or a copy of your official school records showing your enrollment and place of residence.

(21) _____ Proof of residency during the time the disputed bill occurred, the loan was made, or the other event took place (for example, a rental/lease agreement in your name, a copy of a utility bill, or a copy of an insurance bill).

(22) _____ A copy of the report you filed with the police or sheriff's department. If you are unable to obtain a report or report number from the police, please indicate that in Item 19. Some companies only need the report number, not a copy of the report. You may want to check with each company.

**Signature**

I declare under penalty of perjury that the information I have provided in this affidavit is true and correct to the best of my knowledge.

_______________________________________________

(Signature) (Date signed)

**Knowingly submitting false information on this form could subject you to criminal prosecution for perjury.**

_______________________________________________

(Notary) (Date signed)

[Check with each company. Creditors sometimes require notarization. If they do not, please have one witness (nonrelative) sign below that you completed and signed this affidavit.]

**Witness:**

_______________________________________________

Signature) (Printed name)

_______________________________________________

(Date) (Telephone number)

## FRAUDULENT ACCOUNT STATEMENT

### Completing This Statement

- Make as many copies of this page as you need. **Complete a separate page for each company you're notifying and only send it to that company.** Include a copy of your signed affidavit.
- List only the account(s) you're disputing with the company receiving this form. **See the example below.**
- If a collection agency sent you a statement, letter, or notice about the fraudulent account, attach a **copy** of that document (not the original).

**I declare (check all that apply):**

_____As a result of the event(s) described in the ID theft affidavit, the following account(s) was/were opened at your company in my name without my knowledge, permission, or authorization using my personal information or identifying documents:

**Creditor Name/Address** (the company that opened the account or provided the goods or services) ***Example: National Bank 22 Main Street Columbus, OH 22722***
**Account Number** ***01234567-89***

**Type of unauthorized credit/goods/services provided by creditor** (if known) ***Auto Loan***

**Date issued or opened** (if known) ***01/05/2002***

**Amount/Value provided** (the amount charged or the cost of the goods/services) ***$25,500.00***

_____ During the time of the accounts described above, I had the following account open with your company:

Billing Name ________________________________________

Billing Address______________________________________

_____________________________________________________

Account Number______________________________________

APPENDIX

# The Fair Debt Collection Practices Act

## THE FAIR DEBT COLLECTION PRACTICES ACT

As amended by Public Law 104-208, 110 Stat. 3009 (Sept. 30, 1996)

To amend the Consumer Credit Protection Act to prohibit abusive practices by debt collectors.

*Be it enacted by the Senate and House of Representatives of the United States of America in Congress assembled,* That the Consumer Credit Protection Act (15 U.S.C. 1601 et seq.) is amended by adding at the end thereof the following new title:

TITLE VIII - DEBT COLLECTION PRACTICES
[Fair Debt Collection Practices Act]

Sec.



**§ 801. Short Title [15 U.S.C. 1601 note]**

This title may be cited as the "Fair Debt Collection Practices Act."

**§ 802. Congressional findings and declarations of purpose [15 U.S.C. 1692]**

(a) There is abundant evidence of the use of abusive, deceptive, and unfair debt collection practices by many debt collectors. Abusive debt collection practices contribute to the number of personal bankruptcies, to marital instability, to the loss of jobs, and to invasions of individual privacy.

(b) Existing laws and procedures for redressing these injuries are inadequate to protect consumers.

(c) Means other than misrepresentation or other abusive debt collection practices are available for the effective collection of debts.

(d) Abusive debt collection practices are carried on to a substantial extent in interstate commerce and through means and instrumentalities of such commerce. Even where abusive debt collection practices are purely intrastate in character, they nevertheless directly affect interstate commerce.

(e) It is the purpose of this title to eliminate abusive debt collection practices by debt collectors, to insure that those debt collectors who refrain from using abusive debt collection practices are not competitively disadvantaged, and to promote consistent State action to protect consumers against debt collection abuses.

## § 803. Definitions [15 U.S.C. 1692a]

As used in this title —

(1) The term "Commission" means the Federal Trade Commission.

(2) The term "communication" means the conveying of information regarding a debt directly or indirectly to any person through any medium.

(3) The term "consumer" means any natural person obligated or allegedly obligated to pay any debt.

(4) The term "creditor" means any person who offers or extends credit creating a debt or to whom a debt is owed, but such term does not include any person to the extent that he

receives an assignment or transfer of a debt in default solely for the purpose of facilitating collection of such debt for another.

(5) The term "debt" means any obligation or alleged obligation of a consumer to pay money arising out of a transaction in which the money, property, insurance or services which are the subject of the transaction are primarily for personal, family, or household purposes, whether or not such obligation has been reduced to judgment.

(6) The term "debt collector" means any person who uses any instrumentality of interstate commerce or the mails in any business the principal purpose of which is the collection of any debts, or who regularly collects or attempts to collect, directly or indirectly, debts owed or due or asserted to be owed or due another. Notwithstanding the exclusion provided by clause (F) of the last sentence of this paragraph, the term includes any creditor who, in the process of collecting his own debts, uses any name other than his own which would indicate that a third person is collecting or attempting to collect such debts. For the purpose of section 808(6), such term also includes any person who uses any instrumentality of interstate commerce or the mails in any business the principal purpose of which is the enforcement of security interests. The term does not include —

(A) any officer or employee of a creditor while, in the name of the creditor, collecting debts for such creditor;

(B) any person while acting as a debt collector for another person, both of whom are related by common ownership or affiliated by corporate control, if the person acting as a debt collector does so only for persons to whom it is so related or affiliated and if the principal business of such person is not the collection of debts;

(C) any officer or employee of the United States or any State to the extent that collecting or attempting to collect any debt is in the performance of his official duties;

(D) any person while serving or attempting to serve legal process on any other person in connection with the judicial enforcement of any debt;

(E) any nonprofit organization which, at the request of consumers, performs bona fide consumer credit counseling and assists consumers in the liquidation of their debts by receiving payments from such consumers and distributing such amounts to creditors; and

(F) any person collecting or attempting to collect any debt owed or due or asserted to be owed or due another to the extent such activity (i) is incidental to a bona fide fiduciary obligation or a bona fide escrow arrangement; (ii) concerns a debt which was originated by such person; (iii) concerns a debt which was not in default at the time it was obtained by such person; or (iv) concerns a debt obtained by such person as a secured party in a commercial credit transaction involving the creditor.

(7) The term "location information" means a consumer's place of abode and his telephone number at such place, or his place of employment.

(8) The term "State" means any State, territory, or possession of the United States, the District of Columbia, the Commonwealth of Puerto Rico, or any political subdivision of any of the foregoing.

**§ 804. Acquisition of location information [15 U.S.C. 1692b]**

Any debt collector communicating with any person other than the consumer for the purpose of acquiring location information about the consumer shall —

(1) identify himself, state that he is confirming or correcting location information concerning the consumer, and, only if expressly requested, identify his employer;

(2) not state that such consumer owes any debt;

(3) not communicate with any such person more than once unless requested to do so by such person or unless the debt collector reasonably believes that the earlier response of such person is erroneous or incomplete and that such person now has correct or complete location information;

(4) not communicate by post card;

(5) not use any language or symbol on any envelope or in the contents of any communication effected by the mails or telegram that indicates that the debt collector is in the debt collection business or that the communication relates to the collection of a debt; and

(6) after the debt collector knows the consumer is represented by an attorney with regard to the subject debt and has knowledge of, or can readily ascertain, such attorney's name and address, not communicate with any person other than that attorney, unless the attorney fails to respond within a reasonable period of time to the communication from the debt collector.

**§ 805. Communication in connection with debt collection [15 U.S.C. 1692c]**

(a) COMMUNICATION WITH THE CONSUMER GENERALLY.

Without the prior consent of the consumer given directly to the debt collector or the express permission of a court of competent jurisdiction, a debt collector may not communicate with a consumer in connection with the collection of any debt —

(1) at any unusual time or place or a time or place known or which should be known to be inconvenient to the consumer. In the absence of knowledge of circumstances to the contrary, a debt collector shall assume that the convenient time for communicating with a consumer is after 8 o'clock antimeridian and before 9 o'clock postmeridian, local time at the consumer's location;

(2) if the debt collector knows the consumer is represented by an attorney with respect to such debt and has knowledge of, or can readily ascertain, such attorney's name and address, unless the attorney fails to respond within a reasonable period of time to a communication from the debt collector or unless the attorney consents to direct communication with the consumer; or

(3) at the consumer's place of employment if the debt collector knows or has reason to know that the consumer's employer prohibits the consumer from receiving such communication.

(b) COMMUNICATION WITH THIRD PARTIES. Except as provided in section 804, without the prior consent of the consumer given directly to the debt collector, or the express permission of a court of competent jurisdiction, or as reasonably necessary to effectuate a postjudgment judicial remedy, a debt collector may not communicate, in connection with the collection of any debt, with any person other than a consumer, his attorney, a consumer reporting agency if otherwise permitted by law, the creditor, the attorney of the creditor, or the attorney of the debt collector.

(c) CEASING COMMUNICATION. If a consumer notifies a debt collector in writing that the consumer refuses to pay a debt or that the consumer wishes the debt collector to cease further communication with the consumer, the debt collector shall not communicate further with the consumer with respect to such debt, except —

(1) to advise the consumer that the debt collector's further efforts are being terminated;

(2) to notify the consumer that the debt collector or creditor may invoke specified remedies which are ordinarily invoked by such debt collector or creditor; or

(3) where applicable, to notify the consumer that the debt collector or creditor intends to invoke a specified remedy.

If such notice from the consumer is made by mail, notification shall be complete upon receipt.

(d) For the purpose of this section, the term "consumer" includes the consumer's spouse, parent (if the consumer is a minor), guardian, executor, or administrator.

### § 806. Harassment or abuse [15 U.S.C. 1692d]

A debt collector may not engage in any conduct the natural consequence of which is to harass, oppress, or abuse any person in connection with the collection of a debt. Without limiting the general application of the foregoing, the following conduct is a violation of this section:

(1) The use or threat of use of violence or other criminal means to harm the physical person, reputation, or property of any person.

(2) The use of obscene or profane language or language the natural consequence of which is to abuse the hearer or reader.

(3) The publication of a list of consumers who allegedly refuse to pay debts, except to a consumer reporting agency or to persons meeting the requirements of section 603(f) or 604(3)[1] of this Act.

(4) The advertisement for sale of any debt to coerce payment of the debt.

(5) Causing a telephone to ring or engaging any person in telephone conversation repeatedly or continuously with intent to annoy, abuse, or harass any person at the called number.

(6) Except as provided in section 804, the placement of telephone calls without meaningful disclosure of the caller's identity.

## § 807. False or misleading representations [15 U.S.C. 1962e]

A debt collector may not use any false, deceptive, or misleading representation or means in connection with the collection of any debt. Without limiting the general application of the foregoing, the following conduct is a violation of this section:

(1) The false representation or implication that the debt collector is vouched for, bonded by, or affiliated with the United States or any State, including the use of any badge, uniform, or facsimile thereof.

(2) The false representation of —

(A) the character, amount, or legal status of any debt; or

(B) any services rendered or compensation which may be lawfully received by any debt collector for the collection of a debt.

(3) The false representation or implication that any individual is an attorney or that any communication is from an attorney.

(4) The representation or implication that nonpayment of any debt will result in the arrest or imprisonment of any person or the seizure, garnishment, attachment, or sale of any property or wages of any person unless such action is lawful and the debt collector or creditor intends to take such action.

(5) The threat to take any action that cannot legally be taken or that is not intended to be taken.

(6) The false representation or implication that a sale, referral, or other transfer of any interest in a debt shall cause the consumer to —

(A) lose any claim or defense to payment of the debt; or

(B) become subject to any practice prohibited by this title.

(7) The false representation or implication that the consumer committed any crime or other conduct in order to disgrace the consumer.

(8) Communicating or threatening to communicate to any person credit information which is known or which should be known to be false, including the failure to communicate that a disputed debt is disputed.

(9) The use or distribution of any written communication which simulates or is falsely represented to be a document authorized, issued, or approved by any court, official, or agency

of the United States or any State, or which creates a false impression as to its source, authorization, or approval.

(10) The use of any false representation or deceptive means to collect or attempt to collect any debt or to obtain information concerning a consumer.

(11) The failure to disclose in the initial written communication with the consumer and, in addition, if the initial communication with the consumer is oral, in that initial oral communication, that the debt collector is attempting to collect a debt and that any information obtained will be used for that purpose, and the failure to disclose in subsequent communications that the communication is from a debt collector, except that this paragraph shall not apply to a formal pleading made in connection with a legal action.

(12) The false representation or implication that accounts have been turned over to innocent purchasers for value.

(13) The false representation or implication that documents are legal process.

(14) The use of any business, company, or organization name other than the true name of the debt collector's business, company, or organization.

(15) The false representation or implication that documents are not legal process forms or do not require action by the consumer.

(16) The false representation or implication that a debt collector operates or is employed by a consumer reporting agency as defined by section 603(f) of this Act.

## § 808. Unfair practices [15 U.S.C. 1692f]

A debt collector may not use unfair or unconscionable means to collect or attempt to collect any debt. Without limiting the general application of the foregoing, the following conduct is a violation of this section:

(1) The collection of any amount (including any interest, fee, charge, or expense incidental to the principal obligation) unless such amount is expressly authorized by the agreement creating the debt or permitted by law.

(2) The acceptance by a debt collector from any person of a check or other payment instrument postdated by more than five days unless such person is notified in writing of the debt collector's intent to deposit such check or instrument not more than ten nor less than three business days prior to such deposit.

(3) The solicitation by a debt collector of any postdated check or other postdated payment instrument for the purpose of threatening or instituting criminal prosecution.

(4) Depositing or threatening to deposit any postdated check or other postdated payment instrument prior to the date on such check or instrument.

(5) Causing charges to be made to any person for communications by concealment of the true purpose of the communication. Such charges include, but are not limited to, collect telephone calls and telegram fees.

(6) Taking or threatening to take any nonjudicial action to effect dispossession or disablement of property if —

(A) there is no present right to possession of the property claimed as collateral through an enforceable security interest;

(B) there is no present intention to take possession of the property; or

(C) the property is exempt by law from such dispossession or disablement.

(7) Communicating with a consumer regarding a debt by post card.

(8) Using any language or symbol, other than the debt collector's address, on any envelope when communicating with a consumer by use of the mails or by telegram, except that a debt collector may use his business name if such name does not indicate that he is in the debt collection business.

**§ 809. Validation of debts [15 U.S.C. 1692g]**

(a) Within five days after the initial communication with a consumer in connection with the collection of any debt, a debt collector shall, unless the following information is contained in the initial communication or the consumer has paid the debt, send the consumer a written notice containing —

(1) the amount of the debt;

(2) the name of the creditor to whom the debt is owed;

(3) a statement that unless the consumer, within thirty days after receipt of the notice, disputes the validity of the debt, or any portion thereof, the debt will be assumed to be valid by the debt collector;

(4) a statement that if the consumer notifies the debt collector

in writing within the thirty-day period that the debt, or any portion thereof, is disputed, the debt collector will obtain verification of the debt or a copy of a judgment against the consumer and a copy of such verification or judgment will be mailed to the consumer by the debt collector; and

(5) a statement that, upon the consumer's written request within the thirty-day period, the debt collector will provide the consumer with the name and address of the original creditor, if different from the current creditor.

(b) If the consumer notifies the debt collector in writing within the thirty-day period described in subsection (a) that the debt, or any portion thereof, is disputed, or that the consumer requests the name and address of the original creditor, the debt collector shall cease collection of the debt, or any disputed portion thereof, until the debt collector obtains verification of the debt or any copy of a judgment, or the name and address of the original creditor, and a copy of such verification or judgment, or name and address of the original creditor, is mailed to the consumer by the debt collector.

(c) The failure of a consumer to dispute the validity of a debt under this section may not be construed by any court as an admission of liability by the consumer.

### § 810. Multiple debts [15 U.S.C. 1692h]

If any consumer owes multiple debts and makes any single payment to any debt collector with respect to such debts, such debt collector may not apply such payment to any debt which is disputed by the consumer and, where applicable, shall apply such payment in accordance with the consumer's directions.

### § 811. Legal actions by debt collectors [15 U.S.C. 1692i]

(a) Any debt collector who brings any legal action on a debt against any consumer shall —

(1) in the case of an action to enforce an interest in real property securing the consumer's obligation, bring such action only in a judicial district or similar legal entity in which such real property is located; or

(2) in the case of an action not described in paragraph (1), bring such action only in the judicial district or similar legal entity —

(A) in which such consumer signed the contract sued upon; or

(B) in which such consumer resides at the commencement of the action.

(b) Nothing in this title shall be construed to authorize the bringing of legal actions by debt collectors.

**§ 812. Furnishing certain deceptive forms [15 U.S.C. 1692j]**

(a) It is unlawful to design, compile, and furnish any form knowing that such form would be used to create the false belief in a consumer that a person other than the creditor of such consumer is participating in the collection of or in an attempt to collect a debt such consumer allegedly owes such creditor, when in fact such person is not so participating.

(b) Any person who violates this section shall be liable to the same extent and in the same manner as a debt collector is liable under section 813 for failure to comply with a provision of this title.

**§ 813. Civil liability [15 U.S.C. 1692k]**

(a) Except as otherwise provided by this section, any debt collector who fails to comply with any provision of this title with respect to any person is liable to such person in an amount equal to the sum of —

(1) any actual damage sustained by such person as a result of such failure;

(2) (A) in the case of any action by an individual, such additional damages as the court may allow, but not exceeding $1,000; or

(B) in the case of a class action, (i) such amount for each named plaintiff as could be recovered under subparagraph (A), and (ii) such amount as the court may allow for all other class members, without regard to a minimum individual recovery, not to exceed the lesser of $500,000 or 1 per centum of the net worth of the debt collector; and

(3) in the case of any successful action to enforce the foregoing liability, the costs of the action, together with a reasonable attorney's fee as determined by the court. On a finding by the court that an action under this section was brought in bad faith and for the purpose of harassment, the court may award to the defendant attorney's fees reasonable in relation to the work expended and costs.

(b) In determining the amount of liability in any action under subsection (a), the court shall consider, among other relevant factors —

(1) in any individual action under subsection (a)(2)(A), the frequency and persistence of noncompliance by the debt collector, the nature of such noncompliance, and the extent to which such noncompliance was intentional; or

(2) in any class action under subsection (a)(2)(B), the frequency and persistence of noncompliance by the debt collector, the

nature of such noncompliance, the resources of the debt collector, the number of persons adversely affected, and the extent to which the debt collector's noncompliance was intentional.

(c) A debt collector may not be held liable in any action brought under this title if the debt collector shows by a preponderance of evidence that the violation was not intentional and resulted from a bona fide error notwithstanding the maintenance of procedures reasonably adapted to avoid any such error.

(d) An action to enforce any liability created by this title may be brought in any appropriate United States district court without regard to the amount in controversy, or in any other court of competent jurisdiction, within one year from the date on which the violation occurs.

(e) No provision of this section imposing any liability shall apply to any act done or omitted in good faith in conformity with any advisory opinion of the Commission, notwithstanding that after such act or omission has occurred, such opinion is amended, rescinded, or determined by judicial or other authority to be invalid for any reason.

## § 814. Administrative enforcement [15 U.S.C. 1692l]

(a) Compliance with this title shall be enforced by the Commission, except to the extend that enforcement of the requirements imposed under this title is specifically committed to another agency under subsection (b). For purpose of the exercise by the Commission of its functions and powers under the Federal Trade Commission Act, a violation of this title shall be deemed an unfair or deceptive act or practice in violation of that Act. All of the functions and powers of the Commission under the Federal Trade Commission Act are available to the Commission to enforce compliance by any person with this title, irrespective of whether that person is engaged in commerce or meets any other jurisdictional tests in the Federal Trade Commission Act, including the power to enforce the provisions of this title in the same manner as if the violation had been a violation of a Federal Trade Commission trade regulation rule.

(b) Compliance with any requirements imposed under this title shall be enforced under —

(1) section 8 of the Federal Deposit Insurance Act, in the case of —

(A) national banks, by the Comptroller of the Currency;

(B) member banks of the Federal Reserve System (other than national banks), by the Federal Reserve Board; and

(C) banks the deposits or accounts of which are insured by the Federal Deposit Insurance Corporation (other than members of the Federal Reserve System), by the Board of Directors of the Federal Deposit Insurance Corporation;

(2) section 5(d) of the Home Owners Loan Act of 1933, section 407 of the National Housing Act, and sections 6(i) and 17 of the Federal Home Loan Bank Act, by the Federal Home Loan Bank Board (acting directing or through the Federal Savings and Loan Insurance Corporation), in the case of any institution subject to any of those provisions;

(3) the Federal Credit Union Act, by the Administrator of the National Credit Union Administration with respect to any Federal credit union;

(4) subtitle IV of Title 49, by the Interstate Commerce Commission with respect to any common carrier subject to such subtitle;

(5) the Federal Aviation Act of 1958, by the Secretary of Transportation with respect to any air carrier or any foreign air carrier subject to that Act; and

(6) the Packers and Stockyards Act, 1921 (except as provided in section 406 of that Act), by the Secretary of Agriculture with respect to any activities subject to that Act.

(c) For the purpose of the exercise by any agency referred to in subsection (b) of its powers under any Act referred to in that subsection, a violation of any requirement imposed under this title shall be deemed to be a violation of a requirement imposed under that Act. In addition to its powers under any provision of law specifically referred to in subsection (b), each of the agencies referred to in that subsection may exercise, for the purpose of enforcing compliance with any requirement imposed under this title any other authority conferred on it by law, except as provided in subsection (d).

(d) Neither the Commission nor any other agency referred to in subsection (b) may promulgate trade regulation rules or other regulations with respect to the collection of debts by debt collectors as defined in this title.

## § 815. Reports to Congress by the Commission [15 U.S.C. 1692m]

(a) Not later than one year after the effective date of this title and at one-year intervals thereafter, the Commission shall make reports to the Congress concerning the administration of its functions under this title, including such recommendations as the Commission deems necessary or appropriate. In addition, each report of the Commission shall include its assessment of the extent to which compliance with this title is being achieved and a summary of the enforcement actions taken by the Commission under section 814 of this title.

(b) In the exercise of its functions under this title, the Commission may obtain upon request the views of any other Federal agency which exercises enforcement functions under section 814 of this title.

### § 816. Relation to State laws [15 U.S.C. 1692n]

This title does not annul, alter, or affect, or exempt any person subject to the provisions of this title from complying with the laws of any State with respect to debt collection practices, except to the extent that those laws are inconsistent with any provision of this title, and then only to the extent of the inconsistency. For purposes of this section, a State law is not inconsistent with this title if the protection such law affords any consumer is greater than the protection provided by this title.

### § 817. Exemption for State regulation [15 U.S.C. 1692o]

The Commission shall by regulation exempt from the requirements of this title any class of debt collection practices within any State if the Commission determines that under the law of that State that class of debt collection practices is subject to requirements substantially similar to those imposed by this title, and that there is adequate provision for enforcement.

### § 818. Effective date [15 U.S.C. 1692 note]

This title takes effect upon the expiration of six months after the date of its enactment, but section 809 shall apply only with respect to debts for which the initial attempt to collect occurs after such effective date.

Approved September 20, 1977

## NOTES

1. So in original; however, should read "604(a)(3)."

LEGISLATIVE HISTORY:
Public Law 95-109 [H.R. 5294]
HOUSE REPORT No. 95-131 (Comm. on Banking, Finance, and Urban Affairs).
SENATE REPORT No. 95-382 (Comm. on Banking, Housing, and Urban Affairs).
CONGRESSIONAL RECORD, Vol. 123 (1977):
Apr. 4, considered and passed House.
Aug. 5, considered and passed Senate, amended.
Sept. 8, House agreed to Senate amendment.

WEEKLY COMPILATION OF PRESIDENTIAL DOCUMENTS, Vol. 13, No. 39:
Sept. 20, Presidential statement.

**AMENDMENTS:**
SECTION 621, SUBSECTIONS (b)(3), (b)(4) and (b)(5) were amended to transfer certain administrative enforcement responsibilities, pursuant to Pub. L. 95-473, § 3(b), Oct. 17, 1978. 92 Stat. 166; Pub. L. 95-630, Title V. § 501, November 10, 1978, 92 Stat. 3680; Pub. L. 98-443, § 9(h), Oct. 4, 1984, 98 Stat. 708.
SECTION 803, SUBSECTION (6), defining "debt collector," was amended to repeal the attorney at law exemption at former Section (6)(F) and to redesignate Section 803(6)(G) pursuant to Pub. L. 99-361, July 9, 1986, 100 Stat. 768. For legislative history, see H.R. 237, HOUSE REPORT No. 99-405 (Comm. on Banking, Finance and Urban Affairs). CONGRESSIONAL RECORD: Vol. 131 (1985): Dec. 2, considered and passed House. Vol. 132 (1986): June 26, considered and passed Senate.
SECTION 807, SUBSECTION (11), was amended to affect when debt collectors must state (a) that they are attempting to collect a debt and (b) that information obtained will be used for that purpose, pursuant to Pub. L. 104-208 § 2305, 110 Stat. 3009 (Sept. 30, 1996).

APPENDIX

# 3

# Identity Theft Information Resources Online

Identity theft is one of the fastest-growing crimes in America today. Because of this, many government agencies and private organizations provide online information about the crime of identity theft, the latest methods being used by identity thieves to steal your identity, and methods to help you protect yourself from these criminals.

The Web sites on the next page provide information about the crime of identity theft:

**The U.S. Government's Central Web site for Information about Identity Theft**
www.consumer.gov/idtheft/

**Better Business Bureau—Stopping Identity Theft: Protecting Your Privacy**
www.bbb.org/alerts/Idtheft.asp

**California Office of Privacy Protection**
www.privacy.ca.gov/

**Department of Justice: Identity Theft and Fraud**
www.usdoj.gov/criminal/fraud/idtheft.html

**Electronic Privacy Information Center**
www.epic.org/

**FDIC**
www.fdic.gov/consumers/consumer/news/cnsum00/idthft.html

**Federal Reserve Bank of Boston**
www.bos.frb.org/consumer/identity/

**FTC—ID Theft: When Bad Things Happen to Your Good Name**
www.ftc.gov/bcp/conline/pubs/credit/idtheft.htm

**Identity Theft Resource Center**
www.idtheftcenter.org/index.shtml

**Privacy Rights Clearinghouse Identity Theft Resources**
www.privacyrights.org/identity.htm

**Social Security Administration: Identity Theft Electronic Factsheets**
www.ssa.gov/pubs/idtheft.htm

**U.S. Postal Inspection Service**
www.usps.com/websites/depart/inspect/fraud/IdentityTheft.htm